AS BEST I CAN

AS BEST I CAN

JOURNEYS BY WHEELCHAIR
BY THE *GRACE OF GOD*

DAVID FARBER

TATE PUBLISHING
AND ENTERPRISES, LLC

Published by Tate Publishing & Enterprises, LLC
127 E. Trade Center Terrace | Mustang, Oklahoma 73064 USA
1.888.361.9473 | www.tatepublishing.com

Tate Publishing is committed to excellence in the publishing industry. The company reflects the philosophy established by the founders, based on Psalm 68:11,
"The Lord gave the word and great was the company of those who published it."

Published in the United States of America

ISBN: 978-1-63306-531-4
Biography & Autobiography / Adventurers & Explorers
14.08.15

This is dedicated with all my love to Susan Fern Lopez,
April 25, 1939–December 17, 2001.

Thank you, Marsha Portnoy for your expertise and all your work in making this book possible.

CONTENTS

PREFACE

I never thought of myself as a writer. Before undertaking the writing of this book I had never really written anything other than science reports for school. Since my accident, because of my lifestyle, I've had very many people tell me that my life is very inspiring and that I should write a book. When enough people tell you the same thing, you start to think, *Well, maybe I should give it a try.*

I had no idea how to start. One of the very first things I did was to talk to my friend, Marsha Portnoy, who is a freelance writer for the *Chicago Tribune* and a few other publications, to see if she would be willing to do the editing. Thank God, she agreed, or I never would have even started this book.

Many times over the past nine years, I wondered and prayed about what God wants with this book. Was God having me write this just for my own benefit, so that I could relive my experiences and better learn from them how much I owe to the Lord? Or was God inspiring me to write this book to help and inspire others who may be floundering and uncertain about their own relationship with the Lord? Of course, I pray that the second choice is why I wrote this book. I, more than anything, want this book to help anyone reading it to take a close look at their life and their relationship with Jesus Christ. Because without Jesus Christ in your life, you are not going to get very far, and you will have an eternity to regret it and wonder why.

Soli Deo gloria. To God alone the glory.

PROLOGUE

I consider myself an excellent photographer and have always boasted that if the Lord gives me an opportunity by putting a critter out there in front of me, I will get the shot. Though I am always humbled by the beauty of the Lord's creation, I discovered on my most recent trip to Alaska that I'd been a little too cocky about my abilities.

My friend Amy and I arrived in Anchorage on a very gusty Wednesday and drove out to Potters Marsh. There were no birds there, and we almost got blown off the boardwalk. I was extremely disappointed. We made it down to Seward by late afternoon and found out the tours into the Kenia Fjords had been cancelled that day. This put a sour note in my gut; this was what had happened on my previous trip in 2004, and it was happening again. I prayed, "Lord, please just give me the chance to photograph the puffins, murres, and other sea birds. Just give me the chance, and I will get the shots."

Thursday morning was not as bad, but we were given a weather warning and the option of canceling the day's boat outing into the Northwestern Fjord and getting a complete refund or going out and, if we had to turn back, getting only a $40 refund, the same exact thing that had happened on my 2004 trip. Luckily, we were able to complete the tour, though in rough seas. The captain was aware of my desire to take puffin photos— this was my fourth boat trip to try photographing them. In the calm waters of Resurrection Bay, it was easy sailing, and within minutes of leaving the dock, I was able to get a few nice sea otter photos. Heading toward the Northwestern Fjord, I saw many puffins in the water but was unable to get any shots from the moving boat in somewhat rough waters. The waters were much calmer in the Northwestern Fjord, and I could relax my grip on the railing to try and photograph the puffins as we passed by. On our way to the northwestern glacier waters, the captain slowed the boat a few times for various bird sightings, mostly eagles, but I still couldn't seem to get any good shots from the moving boat. I was becoming frustrated. I needed more time.

We got to the glacier, a large beautiful glacier with many waterfalls nearby. There were small icebergs in the calm waters, but no birds. Harbor seals stuck their heads out of the water, checking us out, and I was able to get those photographs. Our next stop was a beautiful roaring waterfall. After leaving the falls, I saw a flock of about thirty or forty puffins in the very calm waters of the fjord. But the boat sped right past!

Why did the captain pass up all those puffins? I found out later that he was in a hurry to get me back to the Chiswell Islands where the puffins nest on rocks out of the water. It was very windy. I could not get any shots in a water this rough. It was all I could do to hold on to the railing so my chair would not flip over. I was getting angrier and angrier and venting at Amy. "I can't do it! I just can't do it! An able-bodied photographer couldn't get photographs under these conditions. Why does the Lord want me to fail like this?" Amy said that the Lord didn't want me to fail. In my anger, I replied that obviously He does want me to fail. Again, all I prayed for was the chance to get the shots, nothing else.

By the time we got back to Resurrection Bay, I felt pretty depressed and utterly defeated. I had plenty of opportunities on this trip, but I just couldn't get any shots. That night, my prayer changed. Whereas before I prayed that the Lord just give me the chance, now I prayed, "Lord, I need your help. I just can't do it by myself. Please, Lord, calm the wind, calm the waters, steady the boat, and please, most importantly, steady my hand and my camera."

When we awoke Friday morning, the air was absolutely still. The tall ornamental grasses near the hotel were not even stirring. We got to the boat, where the captain was greeting passengers as they came aboard. "It's going to be a beautiful day," he said, adding that the puffins would probably be up out of the water today because the air was cooler. I knew now that the Lord had heard my prayer.

Within minutes of leaving the dock, we pulled up to within twenty feet of a magnificent bald eagle perched majestically on the rock jetty in the harbor. With the Lord guiding my hand, I was able to get some great shots. Almost immediately after, there was a sea otter and, with the Lord guiding my hand, my chance to take more great photos.

The northwestern glacier was actively calving, causing a pretty good ice flow in the water. The harbor seals were checking us out from the water. As if on cue, dozens of them climbed onto the ice and posed for photographs.

As we headed back to the Chiswell Islands, the seas were still rolling, but very gently, and I saw more puffins than I could imagine. I couldn't believe my eyes. The captain made pass after pass of the cliffs just teeming with seabirds, and with the Lord steadying my camera, I took a total of 120 shots of tufted and horned puffins, as well as murres and a few other species of seabirds. Elated, I thanked the Lord over and over. I learned a good lesson in humility.

I may be talented, but by myself, I can do nothing. Everything I do accomplish is through my personal Lord and Savior, Jesus Christ. Amen.

BEFORE

I was a stubborn, very shy little kid. I wanted nothing but to be alone in the small woods behind our townhouse in Park Forest, Illinois. At age four, I caught my first garter snake, and from that moment on, I was hooked on critters, especially those that other people were afraid of. I remember sitting in the yard one day when some weird-looking crablike creatures started crawling up out of the ground. They turned out to be seventeen-year locusts, cicada. I wasn't afraid or worried: I was much too fascinated. I grabbed one to get a closer look; it felt like it pinched my finger, so I let it go. I watched as they climbed the trees, fastened themselves to the bark, and—it got even better!—split open right down the back. Bigger, more interesting creatures emerged, with big bug eyes and crumpled wings. Many, many more than I could count, they crawled out of my short reach and made a loud, eerie noise. It was a wonderful experience, and I still have a soft spot in my heart for cicadas whenever I get to see or hear one.

My parents seldom reacted to my fascination for bugs, birds, mammals, and reptiles because at that age, I was more into the just-watching-the-critters stage than the bringing-them-home stage. Also, they were too busy fighting with each other. I suppose that some of my desire to spend time alone in the woods came from wanting to escape the fighting. Both my parents were chain-smokers, and I probably enjoyed the fresh air as much as I enjoyed the critters. I hated the stench of cigarette smoke, and I still hate it to this day.

When I was five, they separated. My father tried to explain what was going on, but I really had no concept of what all this meant. A year later, they divorced. Had I been older, I probably would have seen it coming. Back then, in the late fifties custody of children was almost always awarded to mothers. My mother, two sisters, and I moved to a small apartment in Chicago near Morse and Ridge. Unfortunately, my mother was not equipped financially or emotionally to handle me and my two sisters, ages three and eight, and by the time I was eight, my sisters and I ended up in different foster homes.

I don't remember much about my feelings at that time except being relieved that the fighting was finally over. I was glad to be away from my mother and sisters, but all I knew about a foster home was that I would be living with complete strangers, and I wouldn't really feel like I belonged there.

My first home in Chicago was a good one. My foster father was a Chicago cop, which I thought was pretty cool. My foster mother was a chain-smoker, so that threw up an instant wall of dislike between us that kept me from getting close to her. What I really wanted was a brother that I could play with, but in that first home, I had a younger foster sister who was allergic to animals. I was allowed no pets except for a small tank of fish. Once, I brought home a baby alligator that a friend from school had given me. I tried to put it into the fish tank, but even though it had no fur that my foster sister was allergic to, they wouldn't let me keep it. After barely a year in that home, I told the counselor at the Children's Bureau that if he didn't find me a new home, I would leave. He believed me, and, by the grace of God, a new home was soon found in Skokie, Illinois.

I think I was the luckiest kid in the world. Mike and Clara Burg were the greatest parents I could have possibly asked for. Clara made me feel like this was really my home. I grew to love her very quickly and deeply. Mike, also, but in a more distant way, since he was a chain-smoker. At nine years old, I was able to appreciate what they were doing for me. They taught me the value of hard work and that I should always do the best I could, and they encouraged my individualism along with my love for animals of all kinds. Soon I had a menagerie—garter snakes, frogs, ground squirrels, hamsters …the works.

Except for the hamster, my pets were all ones I had caught myself, but when I was in seventh grade, I saw a really neat three-foot-long Columbian rainbow boa at a pet store. I had never approached Clara or Mike before about getting a boa of any kind—actually, I had never even really thought about it. I came home from school and asked Clara, "How come you won't let me get a boa?"

I think I caught her off guard because she responded, "I never said you couldn't get a boa."

I said, "Then I can?"

That three-foot-long Columbian rainbow boa, which I named Hercules, became the first of many pet boas and pythons. About a year later, the man across the street asked if I wanted his five-foot-long boa constrictor. I told Clara that I would get rid of all the frogs, garter snakes, and miscellaneous critters if I could have the boa, and she said yes. (Later she told me that if she knew at the time when I first got Hercules that boas ate mice, she never would have allowed it in the house.)

Other critters soon found their way back into the house. Mike and Clara loved to fish, and it was about this time they bought a twenty-eight-foot cabin cruiser. We spent most of a summer working on the boat, stripping and varnishing the hull while Clara sewed seat cushions and curtains. I got to do my share of the work, especially running to the deli a block away to pick up corned beef sandwiches and great kosher dill pickles for lunch. Once the boat was ready, we put it into the Mississippi River in Sabula, Iowa, where one of Clara's three sisters and husband already had their boat.

We spent almost every weekend on the boat. While Mike and Clara fished, I hiked through the woods in search of critters. I was already a member of the Chicago Herpetological Society and had been studying about reptiles and amphibians. One day on the boat, I spotted a harmless northern water snake sunning itself on a log, and I decided to try to catch it. Clara's sister and brother-in-law were also there that weekend. My uncle Smitty told me that if I grabbed the snake and held it underwater, it could not bite me. That was the last time I ever believed him—that darn snake bit me four times. After I finally grabbed it behind the head with one hand, it wrapped itself around my other wrist. I did not want to let go of my prized catch, so I was basically handcuffed by a live and very unhappy reptile. There I was, trying to climb out of the water up a steep, slippery, muddy riverbank, soaking wet with my live handcuff. It was hilarious. I finally made it out of the water with my new pet, who, about a month later gave birth to twenty-one feisty little baby water snakes, which managed to escape from my homemade cage. We were finding them all over the house. Clara's cleaning lady found one of the little escapees curled up in the closet in one of Clara's shoes. She turned white as a ghost and ran screaming from the house, never to return. My mom's toy poodle also found a few of them, coiled up and hissing. I was able to catch all of them, I think.

By my teens, the only limit my parents put on my animal studies was to allow no poisonous snakes. I did manage to sneak into the house a small copperhead that I kept locked in my room. I made the mistake of showing it off to my uncle Smitty, who blabbed about it to my mother, and then I had no more copperhead. My mother was deathly allergic to even bee stings. Mike and Clara decided to take a trip to Florida to go fishing for a couple of weeks, and I got to go along. We stayed on the Florida Keys and one day took a side trip to the Everglades. This was my first experience with the Everglades, and it was fantastic. Primal, almost prehistoric creatures everywhere I looked. Birds of all kinds, great blue herons, and great egrets—both much bigger than I was—colorful tree snails, snakes, lizards, turtles, and, best of all, alligators. This is where I belonged, and where, at the age of thirteen, I became a photographer.

Armed only with my Kodak Instamatic, I shot many photographs of great piles of huge alligators. When I had my slides developed, I found that the beautiful images I thought I had taken were so tiny the alligators looked more like small lizards than the fearsome creatures they are. That's when I decided to save enough money to buy a real camera, which I did, over the next two years, by cutting grass and shoveling snow.

Later that year, on a two-day trip to the Southern Illinois Shawnee National Forest with some members of the Chicago Herpetological Society, my fate as a loner was sealed. We were hiking along the gravel road that borders the La-Rue swamp when I spotted my first wild water moccasin near the edge of the road. I ran up to it to get a better look. It was a small, young, very nasty specimen. It coiled up at my approach, opened its mouth, exposed its fangs, and hissed at me. It struck at me a few times, but I was well out of its reach. I managed to finally catch it without getting bit by first gently pinning its head with a stick and then grabbing it behind the head. I gave no thought to what I would do if I got bit, even though I knew it was quite venomous. Friends tolerated my harmless boas and pythons, but when it came to poisonous snakes, for some reason, most people were terrified of them even when they are out of reach or even locked in a cage. I was already kind of a loner, but this really set me apart, now everybody knew that I was nuts. Working with some of the deadliest snakes in the world held its fascination for me all the way through college and into my mid-twenties.

In 1968, I entered Niles West High School as one of the smallest males in a class of some 850 students. Because of my small size, I took the brunt of much bullying from upper classmen, so that year I joined a martial arts club and started training in tae kwon do at the Choi Karate Institute in Chicago. I trained three or four times a week all through high school, though only sporadically during and after college. Martial arts training allowed me to put the reins on my temper. . After a few years, it changed my attitude and stance. Bullies realize that you are not going to be easily intimidated and that you can handle yourself.

Tae kwon do gave me confidence in myself and allowed me to take charge of almost any situation. It also taught me how to concentrate and how to deal with pain by using my mind instead of drugs. I already had a high tolerance to pain, a gift from the Lord. That plus the martial arts training have allowed me to cope with the constant pain I've lived with ever since my accident.

On my fifteenth birthday, I went to Skokie Camera and bought a used Honeywell Pentax 35 mm camera for $50, a used 135 mm lens for another $50, a clip-on $20 light meter, and of course, film. Two weeks later, I traveled to the Grand Canyon with the Young Adventurers Club of America. What a fantastic opportunity to get acquainted with my new camera. I shot about 288 (8 rolls of film) photos in the ten days we were there, a number I remember because it seemed like so much to me then. (Now, if I'm in a special photo shoot situation, I may shoot that much film off in a couple hours or less.) Over the next few years, I added other photographic equipment, all of which I later sold for $400. I added that sum to my savings and used it to buy my first Nikon F 35 mm camera, along with a medical Nikor system for extreme close-up work.

If God has always been watching over me, as I'm sure He has, I guess I have unintentionally kept Him on His proverbial toes. From my earliest days, my fascination for critters of all kinds has led me into the woods to get scratched up, stung, and bitten. This fascination bloomed into a study of the venomous snakes of the world. By my junior year in college, I was sharing an apartment in Chicago with my friend, Karl, and I had a fairly good collection of venomous snakes, among them four species of cobras, a number of old-world vipers, and a growing collection of North American rattlesnakes. This hobby was not in itself dangerous. What made it dangerous was the fact that I enjoyed handling these creatures without tongs, hooks, or gloves. Cobras, water moccasins, rattlesnakes—it didn't matter. I figured, what's the worst that can happen? I could get bitten and possibly die. Somehow, this thought never bothered me. I enjoyed using my knowledge of the snakes' behavior and my skill and speed to keep from getting bitten.

I miscalculated only once, in the summer between my junior and senior years in college. I had just gotten from a supplier in Thailand a small Malayan pit viper, a cousin to our water moccasin. He came in with a bad shed, so after soaking him in warm water, I proceeded to peel off the dried unshed skin. This was the one time for some reason, I wore gloves for safety, and I did not feel him slipping through my grip. He bit right through the glove and got me at the base of my right thumb. I swore at him and locked him back in his special fish tank. Then I picked up my surgical dissecting kit and went into the bathroom.

I called out to Karl to let him know what had happened and asked him to bring me my manual on poisonous snakes of the world, a manual used by the US amphibious forces. Again (because I had been studying venomous snakes for seven years already), I was able to remain completely calm in a new and somewhat dangerous situation. It seemed that this kind of thing was becoming second nature to me. In the book are LD50 charts that calculate how much venom of any given species it takes to reach a lethal dosage and kill 50 percent of the mice it is given to. With this information, I calculated my body weight metrically and the amount of venom it would take to reach the LD50 level for that body weight, compared that to how much venom might have been injected given the size and approximate age of the snake, and compared that to the venom production charts in the book. I have always had a high natural resistance to bites, infections, and pretty much any sickness, partly due to my healthy lifestyle. I have never smoked, and I tend to not go anywhere where there is smoking. I also never drank anything other than milk, water, and a couple of fruit juices. I wasn't too worried about the bite; after all, I had been reading and studying about this sort of thing for about seven years. This was just a test of my knowledge, and the pain wasn't so bad that it kept me from concentrating. I had already applied a tourniquet a little above the bite, just tight enough to slow the circulation, but not so tight as to cut off the circulation, then I made measured incisions into and just above the bite. I then applied a suction bulb to each incision. I had to be careful because of the location. If I cut too deeply, I might sever a tendon or nerve and lose the use of my thumb permanently.

One property of that type of venom is that it also acts as an anticoagulant. This should have made my job easier since I'd always had a strong clotting factor and because the incisions had to be very shallow because of the location. Even with the venom acting on my blood, the bleeding from the incisions kept stopping, making my job that much harder. Eventually, I had to make a total of eighteen shallow incisions, each pair of incisions a little farther up the arm just ahead of the swelling. After about forty minutes, I figured that was about all the venom I could get out. I was exhausted. Making those measured incisions into my own arm took more out of me than the effects of the venom. After I cleaned up everything, Karl and I went out to grab some dinner—Chinese food from a place by our apartment to satisfy the Malayan viper in me.

The next day, my arm was swollen to about the size of my leg, and the guys at work hounded me until I relented and went to see a specialist at Northwestern Memorial Hospital in Chicago. He examined my hand and arm, said I had done a good job, gave me a tetanus booster, and charged me fifty bucks.

Within a week or so, the swelling had gone down, and the arm showed no aftereffects except for a little soreness. Since everything turned out okay, all in all, I was glad it happened. I learned quite a few things from the experience, like don't wear gloves when handling poisonous snakes and that in the clutch, I could do whatever was needed to overcome the situation. One thing I learned was this: the books show this type of venom causes three *x's* worth of swelling, three *x's* worth of necrosis (tissue death), and three *x's* worth of pain. What is three *x's* worth of pain, and what kind of pain? If you burn yourself, it's one kind; if you cut yourself, it's another. If you stub your toe, that's another kind of pain altogether. This kind of pain was like a burning red-hot corkscrew slowly twisting up your arm—not at all pleasant, but interesting.

The only unfortunate outcome of the whole incident was that, two weeks later, the snake died, probably from some illness it had when I received it. But maybe I have bad blood. I don't know anyone else who has ever been bitten by a venomous snake and the snake died.

After high school, I attended Northeastern Illinois University in Chicago and received a bachelor's degree with a premed sequence in biology in 1975. After college, I had hoped to attend veterinary medical school, but I was unable to qualify. I had been working at Allied Valve Industries part-time during high school and college; I went to work there full-time and was eventually promoted to assistant plant manager, assistant quality control engineer, field service manager, and head machinist. My work required frequent travel, and the photographic equipment almost always tagged along.

I don't know if I'm accident-prone or just a klutz. Back in 1977, while working on a large steam safety valve at Allied, I did something wrong and the valve blew. I was hit in the middle of my chest with 350 pounds of steam per square inch at 425 degrees. I suffered second and third degree burns from my waist up to the base of my ears. I had thrown my right arm up to protect my face, so the underside of the arm was also burned. My shirt looked like it had gone through a paper shredder, with me still in it. The skin on my chest was split open, and there were blisters the size of my fist just dripping off me.

My body must have gone into immediate shock because I felt almost no pain. Yet. Everybody in the shop was in a panic, but somehow I remained calm. I think my martial arts training had a lot to do with my being able to remain calm in this situation. Mentally I was able to control much of the pain, but the rest had to do with the fact that my body was already in shock and the full effects of the burn had not yet hit me. Some of the ability to take charge of this situation came from my always having to rely on myself, growing up in foster homes, and also the lack of God in my life. I had to learn to rely on myself at a very early age because I didn't think that there was anybody else that I could rely on. Of course now I know that the Lord was and is with me all the time, and He is the one who gave me the strength and fortitude to endure the kind of pain that I was going to go through when that steam hit me and the shock wore off.

I was just glad that it was me and not one of the other guys who normally tested the valves at that steam station. Most of them were of a smaller build than I and would have been seriously hurt. I told them to bring me cold, wet cloths. Then when they were driving me to the hospital closest to work and made a wrong turn, the pain finally got to me, and I almost ripped the dashboard off the van. As soon as I walked into the emergency room, they started to ask me questions. I said I would answer them later and walked over and ripped open the electric doors to the treatment room. The doctors there saw the problem immediately, got me onto a table, and started covering me with ice. Somehow, I was still completely coherent. My heart was racing, and I was hyperventilating. The pain was now just too intense for me to control mentally. I told the doctors that I was going into shock because I couldn't catch my breath. They gave me an intramuscular shot of morphine, but it had no effect. Finally, after trying but failing to control the pain, they gave me an intravenous shot, and that did the trick. I was able to slow down my breathing enough to answer all their questions.

They got me up to a room where I was put into complete isolation. Nobody was allowed in to see me without cap, gown, gloves, and mask. With burns that severe, there was great danger of infection. Having a degree in biology, in a premed sequence, helped me to know just what my body needed. Immediately I instructed the nurses to keep a pitcher of orange juice at my bedside at all times to replenish body fluids and for extra vitamin C. When the doctor came in, he told the nurse the same thing; as he turned around, another nurse came in with the orange juice. He asked who ordered that, and she said that I did.

That night, a male nurse came in with a shot, and I asked him what it was. He said it was for the pain. When I told him I did not want it, he said, "I think you should take it." I told him to take it and get the heck out. I have never believed in painkillers. I have always believed that if you mask the pain with drugs, your body doesn't realize it's been injured and does nothing to heal itself.

The next day, the doctors were discussing whether or not to debride. Debriding is the removal of all the burned skin. Back then, this was still a debated topic because it leaves the burned area vulnerable to massive infection. I told them to go ahead and debride the whole area because I was extremely resistant to infections. After the painful process was finished, the burned areas were covered with a thick layer of silver sulfa diazine burn ointment.

The accident happened on Tuesday morning. I checked out of the hospital on Saturday morning. Allied Valve had a large emergency repair job, so instead of going home, I went in to machine valves until late in the night. Every day for the next two weeks, I went back to the hospital for whirlpool treatment; after which, new dressings were applied. By the end of two weeks, there was no trace of me being burned, except that I no longer had any tan, and I was a lot more nervous—and cautious—around the big steam valves. If given the chance, the human body has remarkable healing abilities. Now, I realize, God had been watching over me even when I tried to blow myself up.

DAKOTA BADLANDS/GLACIER NATIONAL PARK

In August of 1977, I took the first of four trips to Glacier National Park in Montana. Cruising along on my motorcycle, I had many hours to look around and reflect about life. My first destination was South Dakota Badlands National Park, where I hoped to photograph some burrowing owls and any other wildlife I saw. Since these owls live in the abandoned burrows of prairie dogs and badgers, I simply had to locate one of the many prairie dog towns. I found the area where burrowing owls lived with relative ease, but that was less than half the task. I set up my tripod because I was going to attempt to use my old 1,250 mm Celestron telescope to photograph them. Now all I had to do was sit there in the over a hundred-degree sun and wait. Luckily, the heat never bothered me back then, but it was a good test of my patience.

My stubbornness paid off. After three hours, I got my first look at a pair of juvenile owls peeking out of their burrow. One of the adults soon came flying in with a tasty morsel, an insect of some kind. That's when the action really picked up. Both juveniles came all the way out of the burrow and went through a comical-looking wing-and-leg stretching routine. I sat as still as I could be, clicking away with my camera. It was a good experience at not moving because one of the adults was perched upon an old fence post nearby, keeping watch for any danger. At one point, I looked down, and sitting right under my camera, which was about three feet up on the tripod, was a small prairie dog. I said, "Well, hello there," and he bolted away. The shots that I got were good, considering the lens. I have enlarged some of them, and they have sold over the years, but they are nothing like what I could have gotten if I had had the same equipment I have now.

Over the next few days, I took a lot of scenic shots, including some nice sunsets. On the second evening, after befriending another lone rider on a motorcycle, we noticed a storm building on the horizon. I talked to a park ranger about photographing the storm, and she said that she would like to come with for the ride. The three of us set off to find the right spot for me to attempt something that I had read about in a photography article two years previously but never tried to do.

We found a good spot and pulled the motorcycles far off the road. As I was setting up my tripod and camera, this time with only my 200 mm zoom lens, because the article had been of particular interest to me, it was like I was reading the article right then: I remembered every word—or so it seemed. The storm was probably at least a good ten or fifteen miles in the distance, so we weren't particularly worried about getting caught in it. While we sat and waited, the ranger played her guitar.

When the lightning started, I opened the shutter on the camera and waited. I took about twenty photographs that evening, not really knowing if I was just wasting film. All twenty shots were of different exposure times. All the photographs came out much better than I thought they would. The best was the shot that was the longest exposure time, about ninety-six seconds. There were nineteen lightning bolts in this shot, all black ground and a cloudy, dark sky, with an area in between that is lit by lightning bolts all the way across the horizon. You can see a little purple where the lightning bolts meet the clouds. It has been a very good seller at all my art shows. All in all, it's really my most "shocking" photograph.

I left the next morning for the final drive to Glacier National Park in Montana. The first thing I did when I arrived was stop at the ranger office to let them know I planned to backpack up in the mountains alone. We went over the park maps, and I picked out my hiking route. I chose the Highline, a thirty-eight-kilometer-long trail that runs up and down along the Continental Divide almost to the Canadian border. I set off the next morning, packing on my back all my camping gear and all my camera gear—a total of about sixty pounds. The only food I took was beef jerky, and I carried no drinking water since there is plenty of fresh water from glacier melt-off. I had been warned not to drink the unpurified water because of the Giardia microorganism, but I took my chances. I was not worried about that: as I said before, I seem to have a natural immunity to most sicknesses. If the organism was present in the water, it did not affect me.

I started off late in the morning, not knowing how long it would take to hike the nine-plus miles to the first designated camping area. I arrived there well after dark.

When someone asked, "Weren't you afraid out there after dark?"

I simply said, "There's nothing out there to be afraid of." There was plenty of moonlight on the trail, so I wasn't worried about falling off the side of the mountain. From this camping area, you can see, at the top of the Continental Divide, a notch or depression, which is called the Garden Overlook.

The next morning, the rangers told me that the day before, they had seen some rocky mountain bighorn sheep butting heads up there. I replied that I would dearly love to see and photograph that. I decided to give it a try. It's about a three-quarter mile very steep hike up to the Overlook—and I do mean *up*—so I grabbed my camera gear and took off. I made it without any trouble, probably because all the rest of my camping gear was still down below. It was breathtaking up there. The only problem was that I saw absolutely no wildlife, so I hiked back down. The next morning, I decided to try my luck again, determined not to come back without my bighorn sheep photographs, even if I had to stay up there all night. I got unbelievably lucky. Back then it was "lucky"; but now I realize how blessed I was even before opening my heart to God. About three-quarters of the way up, a small herd of rocky mountain bighorns came around the bend in the rocks and proceeded to walk right by me, some as close as ten feet. I was spinning in circles, taking picture after picture. These animals have no fear of man because no hunting has been allowed in the park since 1905. This was my first experience seeing these magnificently muscled, massive animals in the wild, and I still love it whenever I get the opportunity to see one, even in captivity. I did not ever get to see them butting heads.

A few days later, I decided to try to climb Grinnell Glacier just to photograph it from the top. When I finally got to the top, I was pleasantly surprised because I was not alone. Standing about fifty feet away at the very apex of the glacier was a beautiful, pure-white male mountain goat. I slowly raised my camera and photographed him standing there on the steeply sloped ice with the full mountain range behind him. After I finished, he looked at me as if to say, "Are you done?" Then he hopped down the slope and disappeared over the edge. I inched slowly over to see where he had gone, but he was nowhere in sight. The rest of the trip was much the same, inasmuch as there was fantastic scenery everywhere you looked: waterfalls, mountain goats, bighorn sheep, all kinds of birds, but—darn—no grizzly bear. I never did get to see a grizzly bear in Glacier National Park.

On July 19, 1980, I set off on what turned out to be my last trip to Glacier National Park. This time, I went with Karl, who had been my best friend since about 1969. We had a lot in common: both of us had the same worldview, and we were both agnostics. I wanted to show him all the sights I had seen over the last three years. I kept a journal and wrote on it every night or when Karl was driving. We rotated shifts every three hours and drove Karl's Subaru straight through to South Dakota Badlands National Park. We had to stop at the famous Corn Palace in Mitchell, of course. Though it was basically a shopping mall and I wasn't particularly interested in shopping, it was fun looking around and joking with Karl. We finally set up camp in the growing darkness in a strong wind. Late in the night, it rained.

We had decided to use this trip to get in better shape, so we woke early the next morning and went through our routine of sit-ups, pushups, stretches, and jogging. It was still raining, and the rain really brought out all the natural colors in the rock formations; the air smelled delicious. After a light breakfast, we set off into the Badlands, where we saw a couple of mule deer, pronghorn antelope, prairie dogs, and burrowing owls. There were no animals in abundance, though, possibly due to the rain, which finally stopped for a break later in the morning. We went back out and tracked down a small herd of pronghorn antelope—about twenty-seven, including a few fawns. We also saw more prairie dogs but no sign of buffalo or the elusive baby burrowing owls yet. That evening, we went to a natural amphitheater to listen to an excellent program given by park rangers. We jogged the two miles back to camp, turned in to sleep, and woke before sunrise to an absolutely beautiful morning.

A park ranger told us buffalo had been seen at Sage Creek. We set off for that end of the park and had gone only a mile or so when I spotted a turkey vulture at the pinnacle of a rock, silhouetted against the morning sky. The bird, awakening, was spreading its wings to dry them in the sun. We reached Sage Creek after hiking two miles in one hundred-plus-degree heat. We climbed the tallest peak we could find and, after spotting a buffalo all the way on the other side of the valley, started hiking toward it. Crossing the creek in the prairie dog town, we scared off a great horned owl. I wasn't quick enough, so I didn't get any photos of the owl, but we caught up with the buffalo at last. We came within fifteen yards—he sure looked huge up close!—and got some good photos.

On the way back to the car, we had to cross a small creek. I was busy looking back at the bison when I heard a loud splash. Karl had apparently misjudged the depth of the creek where he was crossing and fell headlong into the water. After I finished laughing at him, I crossed at a different place. When we returned to the car, we found it covered in fine Badlands dust. Karl was also covered in dust and creek silt, including his glasses. He looked like a man in a minstrel show, only painted white in the face instead of black. We drove back into Wall, to the famous Wall Drug Store (which is the size of a shopping mall and has everything you could possibly want, including an old-fashioned ice cream shop that serves the best milk shakes). In the rest room, Karl was able to wash off enough of the silt so that he no longer caused people to turn and stare at him.

After exercise that night, we went back to the rock amphitheater to listen to another program—this time on Indian folklore. Back at camp, we fell asleep to the sounds of someone playing soft guitar music.

We packed up and headed to Mount Rushmore in the Black Hills the next day. We also spent part of the day at Bear Country USA, a small drive-through park with black bears and other native wildlife, though we didn't stay long. The rangers got upset when I opened my window to get better photographs of the bears.

That night, we drove the fifty miles up to Spearfish, South Dakota, to see the famous *Passion* play. Even in my agnostic state, I was deeply moved by its beauty, as was Karl. The permanent set is built of real stone—the town is built against a background of the Badlands—and looks so realistic that you almost feel you are there.

On our way to Glacier National Park the next morning, we saw, standing fifty or so feet off the road, a magnificent male pronghorn antelope. He looked like he was posing for us, and I got some great photographs. Early in the afternoon, we passed a beautiful little lake just as the radio announced the temperature outside was 104 degrees. The pull of the lake in that heat was irresistible, so we jumped in. Nearby was an abandoned house that looked like it wouldn't take a strong wind to knock it over. Even a die-hard, strictly wildlife photographer like me couldn't resist getting a shot of it. From here I was also able to get some good photos of Devils Tower.

We got to the park the next day and obtained special nondesignated camping permits for three nights from the head ranger. Later we took a short hike from Logan's Pass to Hidden Lake, where we saw a small family of mountain goats. The next day, we joined some other campers on a six-mile hike. Karl and I took a side hike through thick brush to try and reach a waterfall. It felt like we were going through a jungle, and we finally gave up. To get back, we could either struggle through all that undergrowth again or go down the middle of the ice-cold stream. We chose the stream.

In the morning, we broke camp and drove to the starting point of the thirty-mile-long Highline trail at Logan's Pass. After stowing everything in our heavy backpacks, we started off for the first designated campsite at Granite Park Chalet, 7.8 miles. The weather was a perfect eighty-five degrees, just right for backpacking in the mountains. We reached the campsite only to find it closed. A rogue grizzly had killed two campers in the Many Glacier campground. The ranger's theory was they were having sex, which sent the bear into a frenzy. The rangers were a little uptight with campers then, but after we spoke to the head ranger, they let us set up camp by their cabin. Later, we hiked about one mile to the Garden Overlook and saw a small group of mountain goats and a male Rocky Mountain Bighorn. We dined on beef jerky and watched a beautiful four-point mule deer walk right through the middle of our campsite.

We were awakened next morning by a noise in camp. With all the bear trouble, neither Karl nor I was in a hurry to venture a look outside the tent. When I finally peeked out, I broke out laughing. Making all the noise was a very non dangerous, but huge porcupine—awfully homely critter, but cute in its own way.

We spent the day hiking. Our undesignated camping permit was good for anywhere between Granite Park and Fifty Mountain, which is 11.5 miles, mostly all uphill and one heck of a grueling hike. We made nine kilometers, only about seven miles in about twelve hours, and I saw my first pika, a fairly uncommon hamster-sized mammal with big ears and no tail. Unfortunately, I got no pictures and saw only a few ground squirrels and marmots the rest of the day. We set up camp on a hillside, but after almost sliding out of the tent, we decided to move to a more level spot.

The next day we finished the uphill hike to Fifty Mountain and took a short side trip up a very steep trail to Sioux Lake overlook. You climb the trail to the very top of the Continental Divide, go over a ridge, and crawl out onto a ledge, the overlook, a 1,700-foot drop to a crystal-blue lake that is half covered with ice. We hiked back down to the Fifty Mountain campsite, then up to a ridge to set up my Celestron telescope, and scout for bears. About ten were seen in the area in the last week, but I saw only one marmot. Then near the end of our day's hike, I saw a young bull moose in a small lake. He was superb, even with his small antlers, but it was too dark to take pictures. The next day at dawn, we were treated to an absolutely magnificent sight—there were now six moose: three bulls, two cows, and one calf—feeding on water plants in the lake. I got some great photographs of one of the bulls with a medium-sized rack of antlers.

We hiked the remaining five kilometers to Goat Haunt at the finish the Highline Trail. Now we had a choice to make: either hike all the way back over the same trail or take the easy route. We figured we had covered about sixty kilometers on the hike up and down the mountains, and I understood then what is meant by the term *tenderfoot*. We chose the easy route—a short boat ride up to Waterton, Canada, then a bus ride back to Many Glacier. From there we hitchhiked back to the car and then obtained camping permits for Upper Quartz Lake.

The hike to Upper Quartz Lake was difficult—all uphill switchbacks, then all downhill switchbacks. Wherever the ground was even remotely level, it was so thickly covered with growth you couldn't see the trail, and we were continually tripping over vines and rocks. But Quartz Lake was magnificent, completely surrounded by towering mountains. We got there just as the only other campers at the lake, a man and his three sons, were packing up to leave. They asked if we would like the large lake trout they had caught since they didn't want to go to the trouble of packing it out. We accepted the gift. Later, we baked the trout over coals and ate it with fresh wild thimbleberries and blueberries we had found. While we sat around the fire making pigs of ourselves, two deer walked right through our campsite, one a beautiful eight-point buck. I told Karl that I hoped the photos I'd shot earlier that day of three golden eagles flying around the prairie would turn out well, since I hoped to give them to Clara for her birthday. He replied, "Then you'd better have hooked up the Celestron telescope exactly right."

In the morning, we went out to climb the boulders around the lake. Last night's rain had given everything a fresh smell, but it also made the rocks quite slippery. I was normally very surefooted, so it was a great surprise to find myself suddenly hip deep in cold lake water. Now Karl had the chance to stand there and laugh at me, which he did with great gusto. Luckily, I wasn't carrying my camera, and the "trip" conveniently allowed me to wash the mud off my boots and rinse my socks.

After Quartz Lake, we took a short drive up into Canada to look around for a couple of days, and on the last day of our trip, we got up really late and had a really terrible breakfast at a diner.

The sky was overcast and raining. Driving along, I saw a hawk fly across the road and land in a nearby tree. It turned out to be a Swainson's hawk, a new species for me, and I went back to photograph it. There were three hawks in the tree—two adults and a fledgling. The adults were screeching and diving at us, trying to protect the young one. I climbed an adjacent tree and got within ten feet of the juvenile. I had switched to my 200 mm zoom lens, which was powerful enough from this distance. Here I was, in the drizzling rain, holding on to the tree with one hand and the camera with the other hand, with the branch I was standing on starting to crack and the adults kept dive-bombing me. I loved it all! Especially since neither adult hawks made physical contact with me.

Reflecting back on that trip and all the other trips I have taken, I must say how much I loved the beauty of nature that I saw. How much more beautiful would it have been if I had not had this veil of denial over my eyes and mind? The sunsets are so much more vivid to me now that my eyes have been opened, and life seems so much more precious than it was twenty-four years ago. Thank you, Lord, for all the memories and beautiful photographs so that I can now, finally, really appreciate what I saw. I wasted so many years of opportunity to thank the Lord for everything while I was out there, for all the beauty He has surrounded us with.

By the way, Karl opened his heart to Jesus about fifteen years before I did, when he finally married.

AFTER

It was in my junior year in college that I bought my first motorcycle. Money was tight, and I could not afford a good car. The motorcycle got great gas mileage, and I felt much more free on the bike. I reasoned that since the bike was more maneuverable than a car, I would be able to avoid any accident. I didn't figure on somebody else running me over seven years later. My mother hated the things and would not even let me talk about getting one while I lived at home, even after I had started college. I should have listened to her. Mother knows best, of course.

I was still twenty-eight years old when I fully awoke from a three-month coma. It took me a while before I was able to really comprehend what my doctors, friends, and parents were telling me. I had been in a horrific accident on the way to the health club the one time in seven years of riding my motorcycle that I had forgotten my helmet.

I found out that a teenager had made an illegal left turn coming from the opposite direction. She had cut off a few cars and met me in the intersection of Route 68 and Hicks in Palatine, IL.

Life-altering event: motorcycle accident, September 8, 1981. Injuries: broken back (T10, T11 fracture dislocation resulting in a Brown-Sequard lesion of the spine, which affected only my right leg). Most of my ribs were broken causing my lungs to collapse, My collarbone on right side was broken, I had a fractured C6 vertebra in the neck, a shattered right cheekbone, and the entire right occipital bone in my skull was crushed, causing a cranial-cerebral trauma that paralyzed the entire left side of my body. The cranial nerve damage completely deafened my right ear and rendered my right eye non-functional. Other than that, I didn't even get hurt.

Odds against surviving the first night: less than 10 to 1

Weeks in deep coma: 7

Weeks in semi coma: 6

Total weeks in hospital: 50

My biggest worry back then was just surviving. I had been a physical fitness buff, mountain hiker/climber, weight lifter, martial artist, swimmer, scuba diver, and anything else that nature offered me. Now I had to learn to live with the use of only one functional eye, one functional ear, and the use of only my right arm. I had been pretty much a loner and an agnostic almost all my life. Now I was forced to accept help, for almost everything, from caregivers and people in general, but I still had to try to do it myself.

After the accident, I was rushed to Northwest Community Hospital in Palatine, Illinois. Though I survived the first night, doctors told my parents I would not live more than two or three days. By the second week, they were calling me Miracle Boy. Then they told my parents that I likely would not come out of the coma and that if I did, I would probably be a vegetable. (I know that I'm more than a little nutty, but nuts are a fruit, not a vegetable.)

I have no memory of the time spent in the deep coma and only fragmented memories of drifting out of and back into the semi-coma. I remember the needle, a morphine shot hitting my leg, then I was out for a while longer. Once I woke to my father, Daniel Farber, trying to shave me. And other times I remember calling for the nurse because I couldn't breathe. My lungs were filling with fluids and needed to be suctioned. This is a frightening ordeal because it not only sucks out the excess fluids through the tracheotomy in your throat, it also sucks out all the air. I felt like I was drowning.

Near the end of November, I was more or less out of the coma, though still having hallucinations from the brain trauma and the morphine. Darn, my ten-year high school reunion was the day after Thanksgiving, and it looked like I would miss it.

In mid-December, I was transferred to Lutheran General Hospital's rehabilitation unit in Des Plaines, Illinois. This hospital was much closer to my parents' home, and they could visit every day, but I hated its cruel doctors and nurses. I was in agony, almost everything broken from the waist up, and all I wanted was to lie in bed and be left alone. Because of the broken back, they had fused my spine from T8-T12 with a chunk of bone taken from my pelvis and implanted Herrington rods from T8-L1 to stabilize the spine until the fusion could heal. I had to wear a specially made body brace whenever they sat me up at more than a thirty-degree angle. Unfortunately, they measured me incorrectly for the brace, and when I was put into a sitting position, it cut into my lower gut. As a result, I was even more miserable, but the doctors thought I was just whining.

Since I was left-handed and my entire left side was paralyzed from the cranial cerebral trauma, I could no longer write. The therapist decided I must learn to write with my right hand. I was still not cognizant of the extent of my injuries and kept thinking that one of these days I would wake up and my left arm would be fine. Nonetheless, the insistent therapist kept putting these big pens in my hand and telling me to make a capital *A* and a lowercase *a*, which is not the way to teach an adult with a bad temper how to write. Frustrated, I kept crushing the pens. And it made me even more determined not to write with my right hand. It took a long time before I realized that everyone was doing what they thought best for me.

In April 1982, I was sent to the Bethany Terrace Nursing Home for three weeks, until the Rehabilitation Institute of Chicago had my bed ready. By this time, I was no longer wearing the steel brace that had been causing so much trouble. Instead, I had to wear a heavy elastic body binder to help support my back. One morning, the aide who was getting me dressed and helping me into my wheelchair forgot to put the binder on. A couple hours later, I doubled over in agony. They got me down for a rest, and that's when I saw the binder sitting on the dresser. Now I understood why my back was in such bad shape. I also realized that the binder was doing all the work, and that's why my back wasn't getting stronger. I never wore the binder again. After a few days of slowly diminishing pain, I have never had any real back pain again—at least, not debilitating pain.

At the nursing home, I befriended Jan Pagen, a woman about my own age who, the day before starting nursing school, fell from a horse and broke her neck. She was a quadriplegic, but because the break was C-6, low cervical, she had partial use of both arms but not her hands. After being babied by her parents for ten years, she decided to go back to school and get her master's degree in sociology. Talking to her did me a world of good. An able-bodied individual may know theoretically what you are going through, but they don't really understand. Jan knew and understood because she had been through it all. On her door was a poem that I fell in love with. When it was finally time for my transfer to the

Rehabilitation Institute, I did not want to trust the poem to my memory. The day before I was to leave, I sat in front of Jan's door for over six hours with a pencil and paper, determined to legibly write down this poem. Well, I did it! And that showed me that if you are trying to re-teach a literate person to write, give them something worth writing, not just make an upper case B and a lower case b etc. A couple of years later, Jan left the nursing home to move out west and gave me the copy of the poem that was on her door:

Tomorrow Is a Dream
that Leads Me Onward....

Tomorrow is a path I've yet to choose,
it's a chance I've yet to take,
a friend I've yet to make,
it's all the talent I have yet to use.

Tomorrow is a dream that leads me onward
always just a step ahead of me....
It's the joy I've yet to know,
the love I've yet to show,
for it's the person I have yet to be.

—Karen Ravn

Karen Ravn, I don't know if you are still alive, but God bless you for having the sensitive heart to write this poem.

The Rehabilitation Institute of Chicago has a reputation for being the best in the world, and I quickly found out why. At Lutheran General, all I wanted was to be left alone. Their rehab floor is geared more for the elderly and stroke victims. I don't think that they were ready to handle someone with injuries as extensive as mine. Plus, there was only one other patient on the rehab floor anywhere near my own age I felt I could talk to.

At the Rehabilitation Institute, there are patients of all ages, some with injuries that made mine seem like a minor scrape, and they were all trying their hardest; that gave me the will to fight and improve. Within a few weeks, they were chasing me around to get me to lie down and take my rest so that I wouldn't get pressure sores.

One day, my next-door neighbor, Diane, and her parents came to Chicago to visit me, and we walked—and rolled—to Water Tower Place for lunch. After lunch, Diane's parents went into the Walgreens store while Diane and I waited outside on the busy corner of Michigan and Chicago Ave. I was in an RIC electric wheelchair that was equipped with a cup holder and drinking cup. As Diane and I chatted, a woman walked up to us and gently dropped a quarter into the empty cup. We just stared at her, trying to keep from bursting out laughing.

The lady looked at us and said, "Isn't that what it's for?"

I answered, "Nope, it's just for drinking."

She turned about every shade of red imaginable.

Later I related the story to my doctors, and after they stopped laughing long enough to catch their breaths, they said I should have told her, "Folding money only, please."

Lady, if you are still out there, thank you and bless you for the kind heart and the many good laughs at a time when I did not find much to laugh about.

Twenty-two years later, in 2004, I went blueberry picking with a friend. Instead of trying to carry around a bucket for the blueberries, I wore a large sports cup that was rigged with a small rope that I wore around my neck, leaving my hand free to pick blueberries. Near the end of the day, I was sitting near the checkout area waiting for my friend to finish up. Picture this. I was in a modern electric wheelchair, dressed for summer, with this sports cup three fourths full of blueberries. I was sitting in the shade just watching people enjoying themselves. A kindly elderly man walked up to me and, without saying a word, dropped a dollar bill into my sports cup. Inflation?

ADAPTATION

When I was first discharged from the hospital, I had frequent periods of sometimes very deep depression. *Why did this have to happen to me? What am I going to do for the rest of my life?* Luckily, I no longer had my fascination for poisonous snakes. It would have been so easy to stick my hand into one of my cobra cages and painlessly end it all. Thinking back, I probably couldn't have ended my life that way because my reflexes for avoiding snake bite had become so honed that I don't think I would have allowed myself to be bitten. Also, my zest for life was still strong. I would have to look on this as just one more challenge to overcome, to prove to myself that I could, and I had a secret weapon—my own anger. This anger gave me the desire to fight off depression and the will to get better.

The healthcare professionals kept telling me that I must look only forward and not dwell on the past. They say you can't live in the past, but I had to rely on my memories of that past to fuel my future hopes, especially when I had not yet learned to trust and rely on God. On my living room wall is a large photograph of the moose I had photographed on my last trip to Glacier National Park. Because this trip was still clear in my memory, I was able to use my imagination to lose myself in that picture. When I did this, I could turn my anger at the world back toward myself by thinking, *What have you done to yourself?* Then I'd remember the beauty of the area in the photo, and I would think, *It's so beautiful, I've got to get back there.* And that gave me the strength and willpower to fight through the depressions and keep going.

It was almost a full year after my discharge from the hospital before I had the courage to pick up a camera again. I kept asking myself, "What if I can't do it anymore?" Then one day, when my Amazon parrot, Beethoven, was outside with me, I decided to try to photograph him. I'd been away from photography for almost two years, and now I had the disability to cope with: it took me a long time to set up the shots, checking and rechecking all the camera settings. Much to my surprise and delight, the shots came out even better than I had hoped.

At first, I tried not to use a tripod. I wanted to prove to myself that I could take a photograph using only one hand, which was okay as long as I used a high speed film and no lens longer than a 200 mm. Soon, I began using a heavy 300 mm, then a 500 mm. When I got a new 1,000 mm lens, I was forced to use a tripod. Unfortunately, unless I planned to stay in a single position, I could not manage a tripod by myself. The configuration of my wheelchair made it too difficult, even when I had help.

I toyed with different ideas for a device that could be attached to my wheelchair and onto which the camera could be mounted. I held brainstorming sessions with friends. During one session, my friend Murray Fisher said, "What about an infant car carrier seat?" Bingo! A light went off in my head. I saw the handle of the carrier seat, and I envisioned a roll-bar device attached to my chair that would flip over me. I took my idea to Mr. Tool, a machine shop in Schaumburg, and Orin, their engineer, helped me design a utility frame for the wheelchair that would hold up my camera and the large lenses. Now I could use my long lenses.

The next problem that arose was this: when my one functioning hand was stretched out to focus the lens on a bird, by the time it got to the shutter release button on the camera, the bird was in the next tree. I needed a system to fire the camera so that my hand never had to leave the focusing ring. First I purchased from Nikon an extended cable release for the motor drive. But the release came with two jacks on the end that had to be touched together to fire the camera. With only one hand, that was as hard as reaching for the shutter-release button. I soon came up with the idea to take the jacks off and wire the cable release to a glove so that all I had to do to fire the camera was touch my ring finger to the palm of my hand.

Another problem: I needed the glove to be loose so I could get it off and put it on by myself, but the looseness caused the contact to not always make contact. Plus when you have the use of only one hand to operate the camera, drive the wheelchair, and everything else, it's hard having that one hand wired to the camera.

My next bright idea was to take the contacts off the glove. I wired them to the outside of a clothespin with a C-shaped copper wire going from one to almost touching the other contact. This I held in my mouth. When I wanted a photograph, I simply bit down on this clothespin. It worked fairly well, though sometimes I'd end up pulling on the clothespin and firing the camera whenever I turned my head. Also, I enjoyed sitting for hours by the Fox River near my home, trying to photograph the winter ducks; in those temperatures, my tongue got awfully cold.

So it was back to the drawing board. I thought about the sip-and-puff systems that quadriplegics use to drive their wheelchairs, so I contacted wheelchair manufacturers Everest Jennings to inquire about it. I was informed that the system cost about $11,000, which was about $10,900 more than my meager budget. I was thinking of constructing a system that would work by blowing into a tube that would shoot a ping pong ball up to hit a simple switch that would activate the shutter of the camera. That's when I remembered that my friend Murray builds pipe organs and player pianos as a hobby. Player pianos work by changing air pressure to electrical impulses. I called him, and he looked in his parts catalog and found what I needed, a simple microswitch that hooks up to the cable release. I attached a tube to it, and when I sip into the tube, that completes the needed circuit. The whole thing fits into a small three-dollar electrical box I purchased from Radio Shack.

The rest was sometimes easy, but more often frustrating. A natural-born lefty, I taught myself to cut mats, build frames, and do color printing up to sixteen-by-twenty inches in a darkroom built to my own design—using only my right hand. The "quality control engineer" that still resides in me continually forces me to try and improve my work.

MY RIGHT ARM

There is a great irony in my life concerning my right arm and a series of mishaps that began in my senior year in high school, when I first injured it from practicing judo techniques with a fellow martial artist. Attempting a move, I missed the correct landing and ended up sideways on my right elbow. His head, which I held in a headlock, acted like a fulcrum, ripping my shoulder apart. Medically, I had suffered an anterior subcorocoid dislocation of the right shoulder, tearing every muscle, tendon, and ligament. After the shoulder was reset, my arm was completely immobilized for the next sixteen weeks, but the doctor told me there was only a twenty percent chance that I would redislocate the shoulder.

At the beach with my friend Karl the day before starting college, I was doing breast strokes underwater. Suddenly, the force of the water coupled with the hard pull of my stroke ripped the shoulder out of its socket. I made it back to the beach using my left arm to hold my right arm out in front of me. In agony, I waited for medical assistance. It was the police who finally got there, and they offered me a ride to the hospital in the back of a paddy wagon.

Paddy wagons have only hard wooden benches and, it seemed, no shock absorbers at all. Traffic was heavy around the beach, and they took a shortcut across a small rutted field, with me bouncing around in the back. In the emergency room, the technician tried to get good x-rays by shooting through me laterally from the left side. Because I had been working out for hours every day to rebuild the shoulder, I was in great shape, and they had a hard time getting the correct settings on the machine.

When they finally finished with the x-rays, I started back to the waiting room, but I was so dizzy from the hours of pain that I missed the door and walked right into the wall. All this time I had been holding my right arm out in front of me with my left hand, and now the force of the collision caused the shoulder to pop back together. Instant relief! And—as they told me later—I probably saved myself quite a bit of money.

But now I faced another sixteen weeks of complete immobilization. On top of that, the doctor said there was now an eighty percent chance I would redislocate the shoulder.

I said, "Even if I just reach out to close the car door?"

He answered, "That's just about it."

We scheduled Putti-Platt surgery for my first Christmas break. The surgery shortened the muscles and tendons to tighten them up. With intensive therapy, I rebuilt the strength in my arm and had no more trouble with it until my red belt promotion exam in tae kwon do. During the judo section of the exam, I went out on the mat with our assistant instructor, Brad, who was six feet two inches and 220 pounds, and a third-degree black belt. I was doing my best, and I thought I was holding my own, but then we fell, and I felt a horrible wrenching in my shoulder.

Yes, I did it again. Same darn thing.

I sat in the office until the promotion exam was over. We finally made it to the hospital, and because my muscles were so strong, the doctors had a heck of a time resetting the shoulder. Also, the muscles had locked up on me. Again I was immobilized and, afterward had to rebuild the strength in my shoulder. I had no more trouble with it until early summer 1978. I was swimming in the pool of my apartment building, vigorously doing breast strokes underwater.

Would I ever learn?

After the usual immobilization and rehab period, the doctor gave me a pamphlet detailing a new surgical procedure—a modified Bristol procedure—that had successfully treated this kind of dislocation. A small piece of bone is cut from the upper part of the shoulder socket and then screwed to the bottom of the socket, forming a bone block to hold the upper arm bone, the humerus, from sliding out of the socket. I had the surgery in December and was discharged from the hospital the day the blizzard of 1978 hit Chicago.

I drove home in the blinding snow with my arm immobilized and wrapped mummy-style to my body. My neighbors were out shoveling their roofs. I had just moved into a new house and knew absolutely nothing about what the roof could withstand. Panicked, I borrowed my neighbor's ladder, climbed up on my roof and began shoveling off the snow one-handed. Soon, three men from across the street came over and helped me. Thank God.

That surgery did wonders for me. I have never had any more trouble with the right shoulder. All told, my right arm had been either immobilized or unusable for a total of three and a half years. Now, that formerly useless arm is my only usable limb.

It's funny how things work out.

GETTING BACK AND
MOVING FORWARD

During that first year at home, I went through ten live-in caregivers, almost all of them turning out to be drunks and thieves who preyed upon people who could no longer fend for themselves. I was paralyzed from the neck down, except for my right arm. There wasn't much that I could do except sit and stare out the window. Though the doctors had called me the miracle boy, I pretty much thought my life was over.

A few months after my discharge from the hospital, the Crabtree Nature Center in Palatine displayed some of my photos, and after a local newspaper wrote it up, I received a call from a woman who was a fan of wildlife photography. We got to be friends over the phone since she was also disabled with advanced multiple sclerosis. She knew I was always running help wanted ads in the newspaper, and she convinced her friend, Sue Lopez, to come over and talk to me. Sue was a health technician at a local hospital, and she started coming in the evenings to help me with my physical therapy and basic daily living chores and the dozens of little medical things I needed to survive.

After a few months, Sue got tired of seeing me victimized by the so-called caregivers. By October 1983, she had quit her job at the hospital to move in with me and take care of me full time. She was a wonderful Christian woman who, for some reason, put up with all my tantrums and problems.

I am ashamed to admit that at the time I met Sue, my frame of mind was such that I still looked for only the physical beauty in a woman, not the inner beauty. Sue was fourteen years older—almost one and a half times my age—and obese. I still thought of myself as the active athletic, weight lifting, playboy sort, though not the dashing and debonair type. I tended to overlook the fact that, except for my right arm, I was paralyzed from the neck down. I had a very mean quick temper and a foul mouth. I was afraid that I took out most of my frustration on Sue, who did nothing to deserve my outbursts.

One of my problems was her deep Christian beliefs. She enjoyed watching television evangelists and reading the Bible. I was so against religion and God that her faith got me angry; I felt she was trying to force it on me, even though she wasn't.

When Sue said she would move in and take care of me as a friend, not as a servant, I said, "Great." But I still treated her poorly. I did not enjoy her company. I was ashamed to be seen with her, and it was not because of her weight or her age but because being with her showed everybody how bad off I was and that I could do almost nothing by myself—something that I was still not ready to admit. Being a former self-sufficient, do-it-yourself loner, I deeply resented this. Sue was a constant reminder of how much I had screwed up my life.

Once I asked her why she stayed with me in spite of my outbursts of temper. She replied simply, "Because God told me to come here to help you." Of course, in my state of blind denial, I scoffed at this. I don't anymore. With her help, I was able to focus my mind. A selfless, giving, deeply religious woman, Sue sacrificed a great deal to take care of me, and I grew to love her very deeply. She was my friend and companion for nineteen years until her death from ovarian cancer in 2001. She gave me back my life and so much more.

How could two entirely different people, almost total opposites, survive together for nearly two decades? One thing we had in common was a love for travel. Sue had never done any traveling before she met me, except for one trip to Florida, but she loved to drive and look at nature. In this respect, we were perfectly matched. Even better, Sue enjoyed listening to classical music, which is the only kind I listen to. Over the years, we took many two-, three-, and four-day trips for various photographic sessions, and we tried to take a major two-week trip every other year or as often as finances would allow.

In the summer of 1983, after discussing the possibility of doing some traveling, Sue suggested that we take a short trip. So we drove up to the Green Bay area and stayed overnight. We had no special plans. Mostly, we wanted to see how the traveling went with me in the van for more than just a short ride. We also wanted to see what the situation would be like trying to stay in motels.

The driving was no problem, although I don't enjoy being the passenger and I'm somewhat paranoid of other drivers. Motels were not too much trouble once we found an accessible one. The main problem was transferring into and out of the wheelchair. Going from the wheelchair to the bed was fairly easy, and I needed only a minimal amount of help. Going from the bed to the wheelchair, however, was another story.

Motel beds are much softer and lower than my hospital bed at home, where to transfer into the wheelchair, I'd wedge one end of a sliding board (a finely sanded and polished piece of plywood) under my right thigh, with the other end resting on the seat of the wheelchair. Then I simply leaned to my right as far as I could, pulling with my right arm with all my strength as Sue placed my feet on the footplates of the wheelchair. From an adjustable hospital bed, this is easy, because you transfer on a somewhat even level. In the motel, the transfer was very difficult. The seat to my wheelchair was a good three inches higher than the bed, plus I was sinking down into the mattress another couple inches. All in all, I felt like I was back trying to climb a mountain, but it hurt a whole lot more trying to slide uphill on that hard wood board, with Sue pushing as hard as she could and me pulling as hard as I could.

Well, we did it, both of us huffing and puffing and laughing. As we traveled more and more, the transferring got easier because I got stronger and both of us got more used to it.

THE SOUNDS OF MUSIC

Music has always been an important part of my life. Before my father and mother were divorced, there was always classical music playing on the radio at home, And I have always loved to sing. I started in school choirs in sixth grade, and by the time I got to high school, I was taking private voice lessons. My choir and voice teachers both said that I was a tenor, but as a very short, freckle-faced boy with curly hair, I insisted on singing baritone, which I felt was a much more masculine part. I had what I thought was a good range, and I sang in every high school group I tried out for. Then, in college, I heard what a really good tenor sounded like. I immediately started working on my range with my voice teacher and eventually became a first tenor. After college, I sang with almost every community chorus I could find, sometimes rehearsing three or four evenings a week. It seemed that I could never get enough of singing classical music. When I moved out to Arlington Heights, Illinois, in 1977, I joined the Harper Festival Chorus, a large community chorus of 150 singers. The group was founded in 1965 under the baton of Anthony Mostardo, a superb conductor and musician. I dearly loved singing with this group, and until my accident, I almost never missed a rehearsal.

In late November 1983, I called Tony to say hello and to find out what the choir was performing that December. He told me they were performing Handel's *Messiah*, one of my favorite pieces of music. I had sung the opening tenor arias with the chorus in 1980 at Alexian Brothers Hospital in Arlington Heights. Tony knew that I knew the music very well, and he asked me if I would like to come and join in for the concert that the chorus puts on at the Lutheran Home in Arlington Heights. I was excited to be asked to sing again and did not hesitate for one second. This was something obviously missing from my life since my accident. Although I felt a little self-conscious at first, the members of the chorus gave me a hearty welcome back, and the concert went great.

I rejoined the choir in January 1984 for the next season. Over the next fourteen years, I missed only one concert—it was in 1986, for Mike and Clara Burg's fiftieth wedding anniversary party. When Sue was diagnosed with cancer in 1995 and unable to drive because of the surgery and chemotherapy, I informed the chorus that I might not be able to continue singing with them because I had no way of getting there. The choir got together a list of volunteers who were willing to come to my house and drive me to rehearsals in my van. It was a wonderful feeling of belonging.

Sue recovered from her surgery and chemotherapy, and things went smoothly for a few years. When the cancer struck again in November 1998, I had to quit the chorus. I just couldn't go there and enjoy the singing while Sue was home suffering. The music had left my heart, and I have not sung since then.

WILD BIRDS IN THE CLASSROOM

Shortly after rejoining the chorus, I was showing some of my photographs to the other members. Tony, our conductor, was also, at that time, principal of the Clearmont Elementary School in Elk Grove Village, and he asked if I would like to come and present a program on nature for the children of his school. When I said yes, it launched me into a whole new adventure that spanned the next fourteen years of my life.

I went home and selected slides from my collection that covered almost all aspects of nature—from monarch butterflies hatching from a chrysalis, to birds and snakes hatching from eggs, to lightning storms. I also showed slides of people working with injured wildlife, and I used this as a way to lead into talking to the children about my accident and the importance of safety and doing things right the first time. For that first talk, I borrowed from a friend who ran a small animal rehabilitation place an orphaned baby opossum and a permanently non releasable screech owl.

The children loved seeing the animals up close. Then I asked for questions they had about any of the photos of the animals or my accident. Of course they wanted to know how fast my chair went or how I get out of the chair. I tried to answer as best as I could so that the children could learn from the experience. A newspaper reporter was there for the whole presentation and wrote an excellent story. This really opened up the proverbial can of worms, and shortly after the story appeared, I was asked by other schools to give programs.

Within a couple of months I had obtained federal permits to keep two injured non-releasable birds of prey for purposes of education— a mature screech owl I received from Willowbrook Wildlife Haven in Illinois and a kestrel I got, on the last day of August, so I named her Augustina, from the Northwoods Wildlife Center in Minocqua, Wisconsin. The owl, which I named Gizmo, had suffered a broken shoulder and could not fly much better than a rock. I had to maintain detailed records of all presentations where the birds were used, including the number of people viewing them. The whole thing made me feel that maybe something good could come out of my accident. I always enjoyed the questions at the end of the presentation. Most of the time, they were the standard ones, but occasionally there was a question that got me so choked up it was difficult to answer. One insightful seventh grader asked, "Doesn't it hurt to talk about the accident?" The answer to such a profound question is, yes, it hurts a lot. But if somebody can learn from it, and if I can keep even one other person out of a contraption like this chair, it's worth it.

I was soon speaking at some seven or eight schools every year, sometimes giving up to four presentations in a day. Working with my two birds every day got them used to human contact, and they both behaved well in front of the children. My screech owl, Gizmo, became tame enough to sit on a perch that I made and allow the children to pet him. The kestrel, however, was a bit high-strung and was all too happy to make a beeline for her carrying case to escape the children.

As a biologist, I realized that Gizmo and Augustina were wild creatures, but when you work closely every day with critters that depend on you for food and keep, you get quite attached to them. In 1995, just three very stressful days before Sue was to undergo cancer surgery, I came in from my darkroom to find Augustina, the kestrel, dead on the floor of her cage. Augustina was an adult when she was brought into the Northwoods Wildlife Center, which had her for two years before I received her. I had her for eleven years, so we figured she was fourteen or fifteen. I knew she was getting old—normal life span for an American kestrel is about ten years. I knew she was a wild creature; I knew I was not supposed to get attached to her. But that did not keep me from breaking down and crying for over an hour. I just couldn't stop. Gizmo, the screech owl, died in mid-1997, with approximately the same stats for captivity and lifespan.

The birds had been to well over one hundred schools and were seen by over ten thousand children. I miss keeping them, and I miss giving the talks to schoolchildren. I relinquished my federal permits in 1998. The schools were not calling on me very much, and I did not feel like I was justifying my permit.

TWO FOR THE ROAD

In 1985, Sue and I made the first of seven trips to Canada at the invitation of some people from Winnipeg we had met the year before at a national wildlife rehabilitation symposium. I had been displaying my photography there, and they invited us up so that I could photograph the great gray owl they had in their care. The beautiful bird had imprinted on people, which made him non-releasable into the wild. If you tossed him a live vole, his natural food, he would just look at it and wouldn't know what to do. Because he was tame, I was able to get very close, even in the wheelchair. In fact, I had him sitting on my hand after I finished photographing him. (Years later, I was reading a book titled *One Man's Owl*, in which the author told of traveling to Canada to meet a great gray owl and the wildlife biologist who works with it. What a neat feeling it was to read this and say, "Hey, I know that owl and that biologist!")

I also photographed a pair of juvenile arctic-phase great horned owls and a young goshawk, who was not very happy about the whole affair. It was a splendid trip: the photography was great, the scenery good, and the people very friendly.

At the same symposium, we also met the people in charge of a barn owl breeding program that was going on in Boone, Iowa. They also invited us to come out so that I could photograph the young barn owls. Sue and I took that short trip also in 1985. I photographed adult barn owls, then a group of five three-week old owlets. After that, I photographed a group of three five-week-old barn owlets, then two seven-week old owlets. I already had my federal permits to keep one owl and one falcon to use in school programs. I was offered a young owlet that was a runt. When mature, this owl would have been able to fly. I turned it down because if the owl flew away, I thought it might be difficult to explain to the government how I managed to lose it.

I had been hearing about the new International Wolf Center in Ely, Minnesota, and talked to Sue about going up there. We decided to make the 510-mile drive. It was snowing, but the weatherman said the snow went only as far as the Wisconsin line, less than an hour away. We didn't realize he meant the north end of Wisconsin. As we drove, we saw many cars in ditches off the road, but we continued northward at a careful pace. We did, however, have one good scare on the tollway when Sue hit a patch of black ice that sent us spinning in circles. All I could do was hang on and yell, "No brakes! No brakes!" Hitting the brakes is the worst thing you can do in a spin. We finally came to a stop, perpendicular to the lanes of traffic. Behind us, a few truckers had seen the trouble and stopped traffic, thank God. Sue and I were shaken, quite literally, but we were okay. Creeping along the rest of the way, we made it to Ely in about fourteen hours.

The wolf center is a beautiful place, and at the time, there were four wolves on exhibit. Unlike a zoo, where wolves can see people, these wolves are kept in an enclosed five-acre compound with twelve-foot-high stone walls. You can view them only from inside a building through a large window. I didn't know this before we came all the way up there, or I probably would not have come. Though there were some fantastic photo opportunities, I wasn't sure how they would turn out. I had never shot through a glass window before. They were kept very clean though, and I was able to get close enough to the large viewing window so that the hood of my lens was touching the glass, which eliminated the possibility of any reflection or glare.

The whole setting was perfect: a clearing of about seventy-five feet with a wooded area behind. The wolves were at the edge of the clearing, and the snow was about six inches deep. The sun was bright. In all, I shot off about four rolls of film, including some shots of the alpha male wolf standing next to a tree in the snow. I call him The Watcher. Another of the wolves, MacKenzie, was the first pure black wolf I had ever seen, and I fell in love at first sight with her. She was beautiful, just staring over her shoulder in my direction with those piercing yellow eyes, though she couldn't see me inside the building. Just seconds after I got the shots of her, the alpha male came over to demonstrate his dominance by resting his head on her shoulders. She moved not a muscle. Both wolves looked right in my direction, and I took the shot called "Vigilance."

When I got home and had the slides developed, I was amazed. They were crystal clear, as if there had been no glass at all. I realized this technique would work well with windows or fences, if necessary. You must get right up to the fence with your lens; focusing well beyond the fence using a shallow depth of field, the fence all but disappears. I have used this technique a number of times and found that I had more than just a knack for photographing wolves, I had a deep love of the challenge of capturing the essence of the wolf, the mystery and the mystique. It is so easy to get a wolf shot that looks like a dog, even though to me they are just big puppies.

I soon found myself photographing wolves at Brookfield Zoo near Chicago, at the wolf park in Battleground, Indiana, and at the Wildlife Prairie Park in Peoria, Illinois. The Wildlife Prairie Park, which has only native Illinois wildlife, is only about three hours from my home, and it is completely wheelchair accessible. Granted, some of that wildlife has not been seen in the wild for about fifty years, but everything is displayed in a natural setting and viewed either by looking through a chain-link fence or by looking over a fenced railing. I've gotten great wolf shots there as well as bobcats, mountain lions, red and gray foxes, and black bears.

After talking to numerous people, mostly birders, Sue and I decided to try a short trip to Point Peelee, Canada, the southernmost tip of the country. This small peninsula of land, which extends eight kilometers down into Lake Erie, is the hottest spot to watch and photograph many species of warblers and other songbirds because this is the first place the birds can land after crossing over the lake on the northward return to their breeding grounds.

It's a beautiful park. You pay a small fee to use it. There is a visitor's center and trails to hike on. From the visitor's center, which is as far as you can drive your car, you catch a wheelchair-accessible tram down to the point or anywhere else you might want to get off. When I say "catch the tram to the point," it's not really the point: it's the place where you start your approximately one-mile hike or roll down to the point. As you look south toward the point, if you take the left-hand trail, it is beautifully board-walked, wide enough for wheelchairs, but be careful: there are no railings or edging on the boardwalk to keep you from falling off. Don't worry though; it's only a couple of inches off the ground.

The boardwalk winds through some fairly thick woods extending almost all the way to the actual point. The last hundred or so yards is not accessible except by climbing over great jumbles of boulders. This is where you will see all the shorebirds you want, by the thousands.

When you start back up the opposite trail, it is fine, very hard-packed gravel. This area is more open, with smaller trees and a few small fields. Here is where I saw the orioles, bluebirds, scarlet tanagers. At the drop-off point where the tram ends, there are facilities, but once you are on either trail, there are no facilities or drinking water; you must carry your own. A little way up from the point is a large marsh, which also has a boardwalk winding through it and is fully accessible. Quite a number of interesting species here, also. People come here from all over the world.

Oh yes, if you are planning to see the warblers' migration, the prime time to go is May 10 through May 20. If you go any later or earlier you may see nothing at all. The other drawback is that, because of its popularity as the hotspot in the world for observing these colorful little birds, you must make your hotel reservations almost a full year in advance. If you are able to camp, there are a limited number of campsites for tents or trailers in the park. When Sue and I went, we did not know that such advanced reservations was needed. We got lucky. By staying a little farther out from the park, we were able to find a nice motel that still had a couple of vacancies. We stayed at this same motel six years in a row.

I have not been back to Point Peelee since May of 1995. The people we met there were all very friendly, always willing to point out the birds to me so that I could try to capture them on film. Everybody who goes there has a common love of bird watching. We met members of clubs from England, Germany, France, and the Netherlands, as well as almost every state in the United States. Sue enjoyed walking and seeing all the different birds, but I think she enjoyed talking to the many different people even more. We saw a few of them year after year and became friends.

After telling Sue many times about South Dakota and the famous *Passion* play at Spearfish, we finally decided to make the trip in 1990. On the way, we stopped in Sioux Falls, Iowa, just to see the river and falls, and when Sue slipped on the rocks by the falls, I got the picture titled "Sue Falls at Sioux Falls." It was a slight slip though, and she wasn't hurt. Sue, who had never been farther northwest than Minneapolis–Saint Paul, loved the Badlands and the stark serene beauty that surrounded us.

At the performance of the *Passion* play, Sue was even more moved than I thought she would be. I was also moved, even though I was still blinded by my refusal to see the truth. How much more would seeing the beauty of Jesus Christ's sacrifice have meant if I had been a believer back then.

A few years later, we took our first flying trip to Arizona, a major trip for me because I had not flown since before my accident. You may say it's no big deal, but there are many concerns that must be addressed. First, how is it done? Do I remain in my electric wheelchair during the flight? No! That would be too dangerous. We flew on America West Airlines out of Chicago O'Hare, and in spite of all my trepidation, it was a great experience. They allowed me to instruct them on my transfers, and they followed my directions; the transferring to and from my wheelchair went without a hitch.

We flew into Phoenix, then rented a minivan from Wheelchair Getaways, a company that caters to disabled travelers. The minivans are equipped with electric wheelchair ramps. If you are able to drive and are in need of hand controls, you can get a van that is suitably equipped.

Sue had a brother and sister in Mesa. To simplify the traveling because of all the medical supplies and camera gear that would otherwise have to be taken on the plane, we shipped as much of the stuff as possible via UPS to Mesa. We visited with Sue's family for the day and picked up our clothes and the rest of our shipped gear. The visit was nice, but we still had a good drive to get to Tucson, where we were going to stay the first week.

As is my habit when traveling, I had planned this trip out in great detail. Every day a different place was to be explored and photographed. It seems like almost everything in the Tucson area is wheelchair accessible, and I loved it. The Sonoran Desert Museum is my favorite place in Arizona. It's a zoo of almost all the different species of mammals, reptiles, birds, and even insects of the Sonoran Desert. I spent a good deal of my time there in the free-flight aviaries. My favorite is the one for hummingbirds. If you are wearing brightly colored clothing in the hummingbird aviary in nesting season, one will fly to you and pluck a piece of lint or thread from your clothing for its nest. It's great to see these tiny birds in action. They seem quite fearless at times. If you are patient enough, you can get good photographs of them when they rest or perch between feeding sessions.

We spent two days at the museum. A few miles farther out on the same road as the museum is the Saguaro National Monument, Tucson Mountain Division, which is laid out with wheelchair-accessible trails. It's a hauntingly beautiful place during the day and even more so at sunset. If you go there though, bring your own water.

Next we went to Sabino Canyon on the outskirts of Tucson. There is a road all the way to the top of the canyon, but no private vehicles are allowed. Either you walk or take a wheelchair-accessible bus or tram up the canyon. You can get off at any of about fifteen stops or go all the way to the top. Whenever or wherever you get off, you can either walk down or catch another tram back down. Sue decided to try and walk down the whole four miles. It's not too steep. I rolled along with her, taking many photographs along the way. It's gorgeous scenery. Some areas have steep cliffs with huge old saguaro cacti and many other types of desert plants growing on the steep walls. A creek with many small waterfalls flows down the center of the canyon, attracting numerous species of birds. If at any time while you are walking you tire out, you can catch the next tram at any of the marked stops; there are also restrooms at these stops. The people we met were all very friendly, and there are many very good photo opportunities in the canyon. It was a very peaceful, beautiful place to spend the day.

The next side trip we took was to Madera Canyon about seventy-five miles south of Tucson, a place famous for its hummingbirds and acorn woodpeckers. I also got some good shots of a bridled titmouse. Unfortunately, I didn't get the photographs of the Stellers Jay, as my electronic flash malfunctioned. We saw many hummingbirds, but I'd had better luck photographing them at the desert museum, where it's much more wheelchair friendly.

Although I take my chair into some pretty rugged areas, it does have its limitations, and I have flipped it over a couple of times. Luckily for me, there were people around whenever this happened, and they helped me get back up. As a wildlife nut and photographer, I have never feared any animal; I love them all. What I fear most out there is the chance of tipping over with nobody around or of a plug coming unplugged. Even something shorting out or any of the million things that can go wrong with a piece of electronic equipment that gets used many hours a day every day of the year. And at the price of these electric wheelchairs, I can't exactly keep a backup chair around. As I think about it, a backup chair wouldn't do me any good if I were out in the field because I couldn't get into it anyway.

This trip out in the desert taking photographs made me feel more whole, more alive again than at any time since my accident.

FLORIDA 1997

With my 1,000 mm Nikon lens mounted to my specially modified air pressure–triggered Nikon F3 camera, which was firmly attached to the specially designed utility frame on my electric wheelchair, I was ready to tackle a photographic opportunity that I never thought I would have.

It was February 28, 1997. Sue and I had driven down to Clearwater, Florida, so I could try my luck and skill at photographing a nesting pair of bald eagles. The nest was on six acres of private property in the middle of a sprawling residential community. It was an unusually low nest, only about forty feet up in a live red pine and about thirty-five feet away from a somewhat busy road. The bald eagle usually builds its nest seventy to eighty feet up in a dead tree, far away from civilization.

Luckily, I have friends who live about a half mile from the nest site. In phone calls, we discussed the behavior patterns of the adult eagles, and with this information, I was able to determine the approximate hatching dates of the two eaglets. I figured it was around the first of February when the eggs hatched. I decided that four weeks later would be a good time to try my luck (there's that luck again) at photographing my first eagle family.

Sue and I got there about nine o'clock in the morning, a little later than I would have liked, because we got slightly lost. I found a good spot to set up about 150 feet from the nest tree; at that distance the angle upward to the nest was negligible. By the time we got there, the female eagle was already out hunting and the male was standing watch in a dead tree a hundred feet or so away from the nest but right next to the road. I got some great shots of him up in the tree with a beautifully clear azure blue sky behind him. After an hour of watching him, I started a conversation with a passerby who had also stopped to watch. He was interested in my unique camera setup, but we talked mostly about the eagles, and I asked him what it is like to live so close to a nesting pair. He told me that everyone who lives around the area loves to walk by and just watch these magnificent birds.

At last the female returned to the nest, with a fish or an eel in her talons. In the deep nest, all I could see was the top of her white head going back and forth, pausing only to tear another bite off her catch as she fed the two eaglets. When she finished, she settled down to rest, and all that was visible was the top of her unmoving head. After a while, the male flew in and landed on the branch only inches above the rim of the nest. This was a much better angle for me to photograph him. For a change, the sun was to my back, perfect for photography.

Now instead of just a clear blue sky behind him, I had pinecones and pine boughs added to the picture. He was busy preening himself and looking around, and when he had finished preening, he started calling. I got some great profile shots with his beak wide open. Then all of a sudden, he bent down and screeched at the female. I don't know what he said to her, but she stood up right in front of and slightly below him. This was a situation I could only have dreamed about! I had been hoping to get some shots of the pair side by side.

I had six exposures left on that roll of film, and they were quickly gone. I tried to reload the camera as fast as I could, but of course, when you're excited and in a hurry, everything seems to take twice as long. I was afraid the male would fly off now that the female was up. I finally got the camera loaded—it seemed like ten minutes, but I'm sure that it was less than a minute. I looked through the viewfinder only to see the female retreat into the nest out of my view. I think I said more than a few choice words. Before I even realized it, the female stood up with a chunk of red meat in her beak and was having a tug of war with one of the eaglets. That fresh roll of film (thirty-six exposures) lasted less than fifty seconds. I reloaded and was able to shoot off two more rolls during that feeding sequence, a total of 108 photographs. Even though I was having a hard time focusing my eyes through the tears of joy at actually being able to witness and photograph this incredibly beautiful event, I got some great shots—so close that you could see the pupils of their eyes.

ANOTHER OF LIFE'S IRONIES

According to plan, the next day, on March 1, we headed down to Sanibel Island, our favorite area. On the drive down, I commented that if I got no other good photographs this whole trip, it was worth it. We had the dates wrong for the seashell festival that Sue wanted to attend, so we left Sanibel after about a day and a half and drove down to Marco Island for the day. The next day was spent at the Corkscrew Swamp, where I photographed a red-shouldered hawk and some baby alligators. The next stop on the itinerary was my favorite of all places, the Florida Everglades, where I got my real start in photography. The second day in the Everglades, the metering system in my camera went dead. With my tenacious attitude, I would normally have insisted on driving the fifty or so miles to Miami to try to get the camera fixed. Instead, I said to Sue, "Let's just go home."

On the way home, we had dropped off the slides to be developed. The next day, Friday, I went to the hospital to visit my mother, Clara Burg. She had been in the hospital for weeks, but she was doing better, which is why I had gone on the trip. I told her all about the eagle experience, and she was happy for me and anxious to see the photographs. I did not get to see her on Saturday or Sunday. On Monday morning, she passed away suddenly in her sleep from congestive heart failure.

I think that this was the very first time in my life that I was really afraid, because I realized that I was not in complete control of my own life. I was not scheduled to get back from Florida until the next evening. The camera breaking down, me deciding to end the trip and go home just in time to see my mother before she died—up until that moment, I had never really even considered fate and a sovereign God. I would never have forgiven myself if I had still been in Florida and not gotten to see her one last time. Thank you, Lord, for sending me home in time to say, "I love you, Mom."

Towards the end of 1997, after editing and printing some of the slides many times, I picked out a dozen of the best slides and sent them into *Birders World* magazine. They immediately published one of the feeding sequence shots in their readers' photo gallery in the January/February, 1998 edition. I didn't get paid for it, but the feeling of accomplishment was reward enough.

In January 1998, Sue and I took our first winter trip to Arizona. We had always gone in the spring, when the desert is in bloom and out of season hotel rates are quite a bit cheaper. I hoped for some great new bird shots because many species migrate to the southwest during winter months. I especially hoped for a couple of new raptor species or better shots of some than I already had. It turned out to be a very different situation down there. The year 1998 was the El Niño, and we had flawless weather every day. I got some great new bird shots but no new raptors; their migratory habits are greatly influenced by weather patterns where the individual birds originate. As a bonus, however, I did get some great flaming red sunsets that are not usually seen until the monsoon season in late July and August.

We spent the first week in Tuscon visiting with my cousin's family and the second week in the Mesa area visiting with Sue's family. Her brother Bud had passed away the year before, so the visit with his family was not as jubilant, but it was good to see them and talk over past times. As always, I had planned the itinerary carefully, focusing around the full moon. I had it in my head to photograph Saguaro cactus silhouetted against the rising full moon. It would have been a beautiful photograph had I not screwed up the plans. I neglected to take into consideration the fact that the Tucson area is located in a valley between two nine-thousand-foot mountain ranges. By the time the moon rises high enough to be seen, it looks to be about the size of a pea.

The next day, my cousin called us at the hotel to say that when he was traveling to work earlier that morning, he saw the moon setting over the mountains, and it looked huge. So the very next morning, Sue and I got up long before dawn and raced out to the Saguaro National monument, Tucson Mountain division. We got me all hooked up in my utility frame with my 400 mm lens mounted to the camera, and away I went, racing out to the farthest west end of the trail. I got there just in time to catch on film this huge full moon rather quickly setting right between two mountain peaks at the western edge of the Sonoran Desert. The tops of the Saguaro cactus are visible. Absolutely perfect! The photo is a little faint because the sun was starting to rise behind me at the same time as the moon was setting, but the prints look beautiful, similar to a lithograph.

The second week of the trip was spent up in the Mesa area visiting with Sue's family, who felt like my family too. There is quite a lot up in that area to photograph also. My main interest was the Lost Dutchman State Park on the outskirts of the Sonoran Desert; with its Superstition Mountains, it's a real plus. There are some nicely maintained trails that are navigable by wheelchair. Even in the winter, it's hot there, so don't forget to bring your own water. Although there are at least two places where water is available, they are far between.

The following April, we took a short trip to show my work at the New York Metro Abilities Expo held in Chantilly, Virginia. Neither of us had ever been there, and we were both looking forward to it. We left a day earlier than necessary so that we could do a little sightseeing in Washington, DC. After getting good directions at the hotel, we caught the metro subway train into DC. I had not been on any kind of public transportation since long before my accident. My memory of the Chicago public transportation system was that it was very noisy, very bumpy, and very crowded. This metro train ride was a pleasant surprise—quiet, smooth as silk, and plenty of room. We got off in the heart of DC, which was stunning. The weather was perfect—temperatures in the low to midsixties, just a hint of a breeze, with bright sunshine.

Sue and I took in everything we could before her stamina gave out. We saw the Washington Monument and went on the tour inside, and even to a nature nut like me, it felt good to see this piece of history. Later, we went to the Lincoln Memorial.

I foolishly neglected to bring my camera gear, but luckily, Sue had brought her little disposable camera, and we used that. We walked and rolled until Sue could go no farther, then we caught the Metro train back to the hotel and had a nice dinner.

This was the first New York Metro Abilities Expo, and though it was a little slow getting started, it went well. Overall, the whole trip was a very pleasant one, and my memory of it is marred only because seven months later, the cancer struck Sue again, this time with a vengeance. Though we had been planning an extended trip to California next, this turned out to be the last time we would ever travel together.

LIFE GOES ON

I wrote this essay during the period of Sue's illness, documenting the many ups and downs we struggled through together.

BY THE NUMBERS

Have you ever thought about numbers and how much a part of your life they are? It seems like nearly everything is about numbers. Credit ratings, how much we work, how much we earn, rent or mortgage payments, phone numbers, credit card numbers—we virtually live by the numbers.

My number almost came up in 1981, when I was hit by a car and given less than a ten percent chance of surviving that first night. Those odds were straightforward, and with the Lord's help, I beat them. Some numbers that affect our lives, however, are more insidious. One of these is CA-125, a marker for an enzyme found in a woman's blood; it's used in determining the presence of ovarian cancer. In a healthy woman, the normal level for this enzyme is 0 to 35.

What brings all this up? In August 1995, Sue Lopez, the woman who I love most in this world, was diagnosed with advanced stage ovarian cancer and a devastating CA-125 number of 750. After extensive surgery and six follow-up treatments of very toxic chemotherapy, the CA-125 number dropped to a nice safe 7.

Throughout this ordeal, Sue tried to remain calm, and with her strong faith, she left everything in the hands of God. She prayed a lot, I prayed a lot, and everyone we know prayed for her. She had a great support group behind her. I don't know if the prayers were answered or if, because of her strong faith, the act of praying and being prayed for removed some of the stress of the situation and allowed her body to heal. We were told that if Sue could remain cancer-free for five years; there was a good chance she could live a long, productive life.

Things were going fine. The CA-125 level was monitored on a regular basis and remained within normal levels. Then around March of 1997, the CA-125 level began to creep steadily upwards. Sue was put on an oral chemotherapy called Tamoxifen in the hope that this would bring the level back down to normal. With this elevation in the CA-125, CAT-scans were ordered at regular intervals, but since nothing showed up, we were praying that the unusually elevated reading might just have been caused by some stress factor.

In November 1998, Sue's CA-125 level stood at 355, and the CAT-scan showed what we feared most. There were numerous lesions in the abdominal cavity and on the lobe of the right lung, also a blockage in the ureter between the right kidney and bladder. Surgery was not an option, so six more treatments of a new and very toxic chemotherapy were scheduled. Sue's faith was unshaken. Mine, however, was shaky at best. I kept asking why, why does Sue have to go through all this suffering again? Of course, there was no answer to that question. Again, Sue prayed, I still prayed—though without much conviction—and everyone else kept Sue in their prayers. After the first chemotherapy treatment, the CA-125 came down 102 points. Thank God! The treatments were three weeks apart, and I prayed, as devotedly as

I could, that if the numbers could come down that much each time, Sue's CA-125 would be almost down to normal by the end of 1998.

The CA-125 blood test from the second treatment wasn't taken until the morning of December 28, when the third treatment was given. A better Christmas present there couldn't possibly have been, with a blessed CA-125 of 49.7, almost within normal levels. What a way to finish up the year!

It's now January 21, 1999. After doing the blood work, the fourth treatment was postponed a couple of days to coincide with another CAT-scan. Remember, I prayed, in my reserved way, that the CA-125 level could come down about 100 points each time so that Sue would be almost at a normal level by the end of 1998. Again, I didn't know how to thank God enough. Following the third treatment, Sue's CA-125 level had dropped down to a miraculous 16.0.

I couldn't keep the tears of joy out of my eyes every time I thought of that blessed number. Sue completed her fourth chemotherapy treatment, with two more to go. We awaited the results of the CAT-scan. She was not out of the woods yet, but so far, so good. Again, I didn't know if it was the prayers or the praying, but God knew, and that was all that mattered.

We kept praying, but the cancer just wouldn't let go. Over the next three years, Sue underwent three surgeries, three sets of radiation treatments, and more than thirty treatments of seven different chemotherapies. Though she got weaker and weaker, her faith in God never wavered; if anything, it got stronger.

At the end of November 2001, Sue was hospitalized after a fall. The cancer had spread throughout her body. Still fighting with every ounce of strength she had, she endured yet more radiation combined with more chemotherapy. The only thing keeping her going through all this was the strength she received through her faith in God, her intense love of family and friends, and through the certain knowledge that at the end, she would join her beloved Jesus Christ in heaven.

Sue, extreme pain evident in every breath she fought for, mercifully slipped into a coma-like sleep on the evening of December 14, 2001 and, after a 6½ -year battle with ovarian cancer, passed away on Monday morning December 17. I can only pray that she was right about joining Jesus Christ in heaven.

Now, almost two and one half years later, I know for certain in my heart, that Sue was right.

Nearly three and a half years after Sue died, I finally realized something. All through Sue's ordeal with the cancer, I had been praying to the best of my limited ability that she be healed. It took an eleven-page letter from a friend that I had not seen or talked to in about a year. His letter detailed the passing on of his wife of thirty-five years. The letter was full of anger at the Lord for not healing her. This made me realize that I had gone through the same selfish anger and fear of what will come next. In talking to him, I tried to tell him that I'd had the same anger after Sue died. I remember the last time I visited with Sue in the hospital just two days before she passed away. She was suffering so much that on the ride back home from the hospital, I finally stopped praying that she be healed so that she could stay here with me. Instead, probably for the first time in nineteen years, I finally thought of Sue first, without me in the picture, and I prayed, "Lord, please don't let her suffer any longer. If you are going to take her, please just don't let her suffer any longer." Sue's work here was done. She had planted the seed of faith in me and had touched a great many lives with her courage while fighting the cancer and throughout her life. I thought many times, was I praying for Sue to be healed for her benefit or was I praying for her healing because I was afraid of losing her, afraid of what would happen to me. I think back, now that I'm a believer, what was better for Sue? That she be healed so that she could continue for a few more years to take care of me, or that she go to be with our Lord and Savior Jesus Christ for an eternity of beauty without pain or sickness.

COPING WITHOUT SUE

My mental stability changed after Sue passed away. When she was alive, there were certain things I never had to worry about, like simply getting out of bed into my chair in the morning or difficulty at night. For the first two years after her death, the caregivers I had living here helped me, but they were not as attentive or as caring as Sue had been. I didn't feel I could rely on them. So I worried a lot, and it showed in my temperament. After all, I was doing it all by myself, because I had not yet discovered that God was there to help me simply by trusting in Him. Since I had lived with Sue almost from the beginning of my disability, I didn't even think I could live alone again. After the second live-in caregiver moved out in December 2003, I was forced to try.

Back when Sue was first diagnosed with cancer, I was frantically trying to put together a crew of people to fill all the jobs that Sue did for me. Every time I had a full crew lined up, something came up and someone would say that they couldn't do it. I had only a week left before Sue went in for her first surgery. In desperation, I went to the church across the street from my house to see if anyone there might like a part-time job. I figured that people who go to church here probably live nearby. I spoke to a man named Jim Hoeflich, who turned out to be one of the church elders. I told Jim my problems. and that I needed someone to fill in on a weekend morning and on Monday mornings at 5:45. I told him what the job required and paid, and he said that he would help me but he did not want any pay. I was dumbfounded. I hadn't expected this when I came over to the church. I had never had anyone volunteer for anything before. I didn't know what to say except, "You're serious?" and then "Thanks!"

Now there are two people who come in every morning, one at 5:45, for about an hour, and another at 8:30 and stays for six hours during the week. All of these people are important to me as friends and as caregivers. Jim, who over the years has become a good close friend, comes in two mornings a week, does my physical therapy and then helps me into my wheelchair. Occasionally he comes in a third morning to fill in if somebody else can't make it. He almost never misses a day. Just as important to physically helping me is that we talk.

I always worry that one of the other two people will not show up and I will be stuck in bed, a prospect I don't like to think about. When this does happen, I'm frantically calling on the phone to get help. I guess it's not so bad when I'm stuck in bed. I'll survive. But on mornings when we have done medical procedures and I'm stuck in my uncomfortable shower/commode chair for hours, its more than just painful. With that hard seat, there is a high risk of pressure sores. I had one on my right buttocks that wouldn't close for over two and a half years, and I finally spent three weeks in the hospital last June, 2003 to get it fixed with surgery. I do not like the thought of going through that again.

There are so many little things that are taken for granted because we do them naturally without even thinking. When you can no longer even get dressed by yourself or even change position in your chair by yourself, that's when you really appreciate what you lost.

Again, I need to learn to trust in the Lord more and not worry so much.

DISABILITIES—A NEW VIEWPOINT

I had a revelation the other day that made me so happy it brought tears to my eyes. First let me explain that I have always felt uncomfortable around mentally challenged individuals.

Some of that discomfort comes from my inability to understand anyone who does not speak clearly. (Hearing in my left ear was already greatly reduced from noises I was subjected to before the accident, and brain trauma destroyed the auditory nerve to my right ear.) Part of my discomfort comes from thinking that I have an unusually sharp mind, although I can rarely even remember what day it is. (My cognitive ability was affected slightly by the brain trauma, but I still can't forget a lousy joke if I hear one, and that really clutters up the memory space.)

Anyway, from time to time, I work on a special project with a good friend of mine, Dr. Murray Fisher, who teaches special education at the Southside Occupational Academy, a high school for mentally challenged individuals. He also teaches psychology of the exceptional child at various colleges and universities. He first taught this graduate-level course in the mid-1980s at Northeastern Illinois University, where we had once been students. When Murray asked if I would like to help him teach teachers what it's like to be disabled, I jumped at the chance.

During the second class of the session, students chose a disability to cope with. Some wore special glasses to simulate tunnel vision or cataracts. Some went blindfolded to simulate various stages of blindness; some wore their arm in slings. A few put wet cotton in their ears to simulate deafness; a few wore special gloves with thumbs and fingers sewn together to simulate severe arthritis. One or two chose to go in wheelchairs. They teamed up, and we went on a short trip to the student union, an ideal place because there are several steps leading down to it. There is a ramp, but as you go down it, on the right side is a stucco wall, rather hard on the knuckles. I showed the students how to help each other up or down the stairs in the wheelchair in the event that there might be no ramp.

As the students tried to help each other fish coins out of pockets, use vending machines and navigate through bathroom doors, they got a small taste of the difficulty of being disabled in an able-bodied world. After the field trip, we went back to the classroom for a discussion of their feelings and frustrations. That's when I got up to speak.

I tried to fill them in on what almost everyone who becomes disabled—either by accident or sickness, by an acquired disability or by a congenital birth defect—goes through: the six stages, which are denial, bargaining, anger, frustration, depression, and acceptance. After my little talk, I invited them to ask questions. "Don't worry," I said, "I'm a biologist. There is nothing you can ask that will embarrass me."

The students, normally veteran teachers taking this course to be recertified in Illinois, were slow at first to ask anything personal, but after a few questions, they warmed up to the task. It was a great feeling for me to be able to help someone learn from my accident; the experience gave me, as a disabled person, a whole new outlook on life.

We conducted this session every semester for a number of years at Northeastern Illinois University as well as at a few other universities. After a hiatus of a few years, we held a session at DePaul University again on June 29, 2004, but for the first time as an undergraduate course. It was also the first day of summer school at the Southside Academy. I rode down to the academy with Murray so we could just go straight to DePaul after his morning classes. Before classes began, I was sitting out in the hallway waiting for him to finish some paperwork and collect his pupils. One of the other teachers had formed four of the young men into a cleaning crew, wiping down the hall lockers. As I watched them, I saw that they were really trying to do a good job and even seemed to be enjoying it. I started thinking, would a nonchallenged teenager do as good a job on such a menial task, or would they just slough it off as beneath them. Would I have done as well? Or would I have told them to get someone else?

As I sat there pondering, I said to myself, *David, you can't even do what those students are doing*. For the first time, I realized that everybody has his or her strong points. Afterward, sitting in the class, I felt completely comfortable in spite of my hearing difficulties. I also realized how someone with an IQ as high as Murray's could love teaching at a school for the mentally challenged. Unlike a regular high school where, as I remember, where many students don't even want to be there and everything is rushed and jittery, the atmosphere in this school was one of calmness. The students all seemed to be enjoying themselves, and they were giving it all they had. I felt like a whole wall inside my brain had come tumbling down.

By what definition is a person considered mentally impaired? If that person is born a slow learner but performs his or her best at any task and trusts everybody naturally? If that person is born with "normal" learning abilities, has studied as much as I have, taught myself all the intricacies of photography, loves nature almost to the point of worship, but takes fifty years to admit to himself that everything was created by the Almighty God? Now I can appreciate people better for who they are inside, rather than for how they appear on the outside.

When Murray and I got to DePaul University later that day, I could not believe what I saw! A modern, state-of-the-art classroom building set on a beautiful campus in the middle of Chicago, with a central lounge where students or nonstudents can meet. The only problem is you have to go down two steps to get there. But! They forgot to provide a ramp, so the area is inaccessible to anyone in a wheelchair.

GOD AND ME

Why was I born with a heart so hardened against God, even before I had any concept of God? At the age of five, after the first day of Hebrew school, I told my father I wouldn't go back and he couldn't make me, although I'm sure he could have. I have vague memories of him lighting the Hanukkah menorah while saying the Hebrew prayer and of my mother blessing the Sabbath candles. Children are supposed to be products of their environments, but my parents didn't force the issue.

I don't understand how I could have been so blind and stupid about matters concerning religion in general and God in particular. Since my earliest days, I believed in the sciences. I refused to let myself even think about the existence of an Almighty God. But I must have at least deep down believed in Him much of my denial and resistance must have been my fear of admitting that I was wrong all those years and having to face up for all my sins.

I found myself trying to bargain with Him after the accident, when I first came out of the coma. I would be good and do anything He wanted me to do if only I could just move my left arm or my legs again.

A few years before Sue passed away, she had given me a very nice Bible. Whenever she or anybody else said that I should read this Psalm or such and such passage, my response was always the same: "I will, one of these days." Finally, about a year and a half after Sue's death, I said to myself, "No more 'one of these days,'" and I started to read the Bible—not just passages, but cover to cover, both Old and New Testament. I had been going to the church across the street from my house more or less regularly. It is a small congregation of about twenty people, and I felt comfortable with them as my extended family. They were interested in the progress of my Bible reading. We discussed the many questions that would come up.

I was starting on the New Testament when my caregiver and I left for Alaska in November 2003. I wanted to find out what it was that made people believers. I was already somewhat familiar with the New Testament from my thirty or so years of singing classical choral music—much of which was written for the church—and because of Sue. It was slow reading at first because I didn't want to let go of my old ways, but I plowed on and learned. Before I had even finished the book of Acts, I knew I had to have Christ in my life. It wasn't that I suddenly started to believe, but more that I very much wanted to believe because I finally realized that something vital in my life was missing. So on Christmas Day 2003, I confessed my sins and asked Christ to enter into my life, accepting Him as the Messiah that God had promised to send since the beginning of the Old Testament.

Now, I live as best a Christian life as I can without abandoning the Judaism that is my root culture. Now I more than just want to believe. Enough has happened in my life to make me a firm believer, and thanks to my inborn stubbornness, I have a resolve that makes my belief and my desire to learn more about God even greater. Since I became a believer, I have had a few revelations to questions in my mind. I would like to think that I figured out the answers by myself, but I'm just not that bright.

When I started writing this book more than five years ago, in 2003, I was still an agnostic. I still believed only in the sciences and with Darwin's theory of evolution and natural selection. At the very beginning of this book and this chapter, I mentioned that even as a very young child, my heart was hardened against the Lord, even before I really had any concept of the Lord. Why? Yesterday, December 17, 2008, at the end of our weekly Bible study, I received the answer to my question about why I was that way. As a young child I was very curious about where everything in nature came from and how they worked. I had been told that God created everything, but I couldn't accept that. It was just too simple.

In my very limited knowledge, combined with my total ignorance of who God really is, I thought of God within my own very limited human abilities. I certainly couldn't create a weed, let alone a tree or a butterfly, although I do occasionally create a mess. My dad couldn't create a frog or anything else either, so how could God? I was so full of unanswered questions that I embraced the sciences and probably just about any other foolish ideas that answered, however incorrectly, my questions. I can now fully accept that God created all things and that nothing living just happened without the supreme hand and knowledge of the Lord molding and shaping it.

I feel like a great curtain has finally been removed from over my eyes and heart. I still do believe, at least a little, in evolution. Things and traits, within a species gene pool do change over a long enough period of time, but that would be microevolution and mostly adaptations for survival. I do not believe that a reptile could ever evolve into, say, a bird.

Even though some people still act as ignorant as an ape like creature, I no longer believe that man evolved from anything that was apelike. God created man in His own image.

One such revelation was about Communion, the passing the bread and drink. In Matthew 26:26, Jesus took bread, blessed and broke it, and gave it to the disciples, and said, "Take, eat; this is My body." And then in Matthew 26:27–28 it reads, "Then He took the cup, and gave thanks, and gave it to them, saying, 'Drink from it, all of you." for this is My blood of the new covenant, which is shed for many for the remission of sins. [NKJV]

I could understand why so many people have trouble with this. It doesn't sound very appealing. I was brushing my teeth one evening, and the answer came to me as clear as a bell, and I hadn't even been thinking about it.

When Christ said, "Take, eat, this is My body," he wasn't speaking about his body in the literal physical sense. He was speaking about his spiritual body, the body and flesh of the New Covenant. This is best explained in John 6:33,35: "For the bread of God is He who comes down from heaven, and gives life to the world." And Jesus said to them, "I am the bread of life. He who comes to Me shall never hunger, and he who believes in Me shall never thirst.

When you eat something and digest it, you absorb it into your system, it becomes part of you, no longer something separate from you. You can never get rid of it or lose it. In this case, the spirit of Christ is with you until the very end. Drinking His blood—the blood of the New Covenant—washes away all your sins and gives you a fresh start if you believe in and accept Christ into your life.

In John 20:29, Jesus said to Thomas, "Blessed are those that have not seen and yet have believed." We just have to take it on faith that when we receive Communion we are eating His flesh, the Bread of Life, the body and flesh of the New Testament. The next Sunday at church, I took my first Communion, and a small drink and piece of bread never tasted so good.

Why did I have this accident? Was it truly just an accident that nobody, not even God, had any control of? I don't think so. God gave man control over himself, but He still knows and controls everything that happens or is going to happen. Back in February 2004, I was having one of my usual restless nights, so I was reading the Bible. I'm pretty sure it was somewhere in the book of Kings 1 that something clicked inside of me, and all of a sudden, I felt I knew exactly why I had the accident. When I awoke the next morning, I thanked God for the accident and for my surviving. My accident was not a punishment: it was a wake-up call. God knew that my lifestyle was fatalistic, leading me toward disaster. I'd been handling the deadliest snakes without any precautions, climbing or hiking in mountains by myself using no safety equipment, riding motorcycles, doing just about anything that was dangerous. Sooner or later, I would have either gotten bitten fatally, or crashed, or fallen somewhere alone and died.

That by itself is no big deal, except that I would have died without ever knowing or accepting God's grace by the sacrifice of His only son, Jesus Christ for our salvation. God does not want that to happen. He does not want to lose even one soul. I had never done anything so morally wrong that I could not still be saved by simply accepting Christ into my life.

The more I think about it, the more I realize that even if I could, I would not change anything except the pain I caused others. I definitely would like to have spared my parents and friends the worry and anguish they went through while sitting by my bedside for those first three months. Even before I found God and accepted Christ, I don't think I would have changed anything because of all the wonderful new friends I have made since my accident. Plus I have a whole new outlook now. Before the accident, I worked fifty to sixty or more hours a week, many of which were out of town. My photography was basically a hobby, even though I had plans to build a darkroom in the home I bought when I was twenty-five years old. I may never have gotten around to it because money was always a problem. Looking back, I would probably still be working my life away—that is, if I were still alive. I never would have met Sue and had nineteen years of her love and learned how to love in return. There's just so much I never would have experienced and so many people that I hold very dear to me now who I never would have met.

I don't thank God for everything as often as I should because it's not second nature for me yet, but whenever I think about it, which is quite often, I thank God for everything including and especially for my accident. I needed this second chance to learn what life is really all about. It's not just about biology. Although we do live in a body that is flesh and blood, it's a spiritual life not to be squandered away without God's grace.

I don't remember that I have really ever been bitter about my accident, though I know that I wasn't happy about it. Over the years, I have often wondered if my lifestyle was so bad that God would punish me like this. If God were a vindictive and vengeful God, then, yes, I probably deserved what I got simply for denying Him. Since I started reading the Bible, I realize that God is a jealous God, but He is not vindictive or vengeful. Vengeful would have been a heck of a lot worse than this.

Whenever people I've just met ask about the accident, after I tell them, they usually say, "How terrible." The funny thing is that I no longer view my accident as terrible but as possibly the best thing that ever happened to me. It was a second chance at living and learning what life is really all about.

I liked parts of my previous life, but that's because I didn't know any better. I was blind to the truth. I certainly could not go back to that godless lifestyle now even if I were physically capable of doing so.

I never got married, and I don't think I ever really came close. As a child, I had witnessed the bad scene at home during the separation and subsequent divorce of my parents, and I think I decided then never to get married. Most of my relationships were based only upon physical attraction, on lust, not the sort of thing you can build a marriage on. I always told myself I never found the right woman, or I didn't have the time for a relationship. The truth is that I was just immature, afraid to make that kind of commitment to somebody because I didn't think I could live up to it.

Before my accident, I don't think I even knew how to love, how to really give of myself. It took almost nineteen years of living with Sue before I was able to genuinely care about and love someone else. If you find yourself in a similar situation, read the Bible. All the answers are in there, as long as you read with your heart as well as with your mind and your eyes. You must first open your heart to God before you can truly open your heart to anyone else. I hope that at this late stage in my life, if I ever get the chance again, maybe I can still find my soul mate, someone I want to spend the rest of my mortal life with purely for the enjoyment of being with her.

I feel calmer now that I trust in God. When I have done my best, and that's not quite enough, if it's meant to be, I believe God will fix the problem for me. Also, life is much simpler now because there are fewer choices to be made. When it comes to behavior and how you act in different situations, there really is only one right way to act. Think with your head and heart. Don't, as I did in the past, let your body and physical desires do your thinking for you.

MIRACLES AND ALASKA

NORTH TO ALASKA—THE FIRST TIME

Planning trips in detail and traveling to different places to photograph the beautiful scenery and all God's creatures great and small are the things that kept me going over the years since my accident. As far back as I can remember, after watching TV shows about the wildlife and natural beauty of Alaska, I have had a burning desire to travel there to see and photograph everything I could. Unfortunately, like many dreams, this one had to be put on the back burner. There was never enough time or money.

Finally, twenty-one years after my accident, I'd reawakened the dream. Actually, I don't think I'd ever really given up on it, but I realized that, given my temperament, I could never have even planned this trip before I accepted God into my life. I first had to learn to trust in the Lord. Maybe it was His idea that I go. Maybe just believing gave me the confidence to tackle a journey of this magnitude.

I had no way of knowing it then, but all the planning I did to make this dream a reality would not be nearly enough. I had to depend, ultimately, on the miracles that were waiting for me.

My plan had always been to take a six-week driving trip, and I had three objectives in mind. Number one, to photograph the Chilkat Valley, which had been designated a national bald eagle preserve in June of 1982 while I was recovering in the hospital. I also wanted to see Denali National Park. The third and most challenging objective was the Brooks Camp at the Katmai National Park on the peninsula at the base of the Aleutian Islands where, I hoped, I'd be able to observe and photograph the great coastal Alaska brown bears, grizzlies, in the wild.

After sending a great many e-mails, making dozens of phone calls, and reading extensively, I discovered that all three places could not possibly be seen at their best in a single trip unless that trip lasted from July through December. In late September 2003, I spoke to Joel Telford, head ranger at the Chilkat Valley Bald Eagle Preserve, who told me the best time to see large concentrations of eagles was mid-November into December. Eagles congregate in a small part of the valley called the Council Grounds because when the rest of Alaska is frozen over, in this area there is an upwelling of underground water that keeps the river open, making it ideal for the late-spawning chum salmon. Eagles migrate there from the surrounding one hundred thousand square miles and stay as long as the salmon hold out. Within an hour of talking to Joel, I started formulating a plan to go to Alaska that November.

It was amazing to me that I could change my entire itinerary so quickly and clearheadedly. Now all I had to do was make another great many phone calls and e-mails. To get from Juneau to Haines, I had to coordinate the plane flight with the ferry schedule, which only runs a couple of times a week in the winter. I had to arrange for transportation from the airport to the hotel once we got to Juneau, and then from the hotel to the ferry. Once we arrived in Haines, I would have to find somewhere to stay that could accommodate my electric wheelchair and arrange for transportation around town and to the Chilkat Valley Bald Eagle Preserve. Everybody up there was very helpful in my endeavor;

everybody I talked to gave me other contacts to talk to. Within a few days, I was able to piece together enough information and contacts to begin planning the trip in earnest. Ruby De Luna of South East Alaska Independent Living arranged for transportation from the hotel to the ferry terminal, then got a volunteer to pick us up from the ferry terminal at nine o'clock on the Sunday evening of our return to Juneau.

Through Joel Telford, I had gotten the name of the director of the Bald Eagle Foundation. David Olerud is a paraplegic who has been confined to a wheelchair for thirty years and has lived in Haines all that time. He was more than happy to provide me with the names of hotels and bed-and-breakfast places he thought could accommodate my electric wheelchair. Not surprisingly, in the very small town of Haines, there are only a few. We stayed at the On the Beach Inn B & B a renovated home that is nicely ramped for wheelchair access, right on the beautiful Lynn Canal. Owners Gary and Jane Hall are more than just proprietors; they are good Christian people and good friends. Jane is also a marvelous cook.

David Olerud also provided me with the name of a business that arranges tours of the bald eagle preserve. Alaska Nature tours, owned and operated by Dan Egolf, was able to get the use of a bus equipped with a wheelchair lift. Dan turned out to be more than helpful and extra friendly.

For those of you who are confined to a wheelchair and have not traveled by plane, here is how it happens. I go through the search like everyone else nowadays. Since I can't walk through the metal detectors, the security people use a handheld detector and mirrors to check all around and under my electric wheelchair. Wheelchair passengers are first to board and last to leave. At boarding time, I roll right up to the door of the plane on the extending walkway from the terminal, then the flight attendants pick me up and transfer me to a special aisle chair, a very narrow chair on wheels, then they wheel me to my seat and lift me into it. At the end of the flight, the whole process is reversed, and my wheelchair, which was stowed in the hull of the plane after I had been transferred, is usually waiting by the door of the plane by the time the flight attendants get me off.

The night before I was to leave, my mind was racing, and I couldn't sleep. I didn't even feel tired. I lay in bed listening to music and reading the *Milepost*, a magazine that gives a mile-by-mile breakdown of the major road routes and highways in Alaska. What got me so completely excited was an ad I came across while reading about the town of Valdez and the route into it. Two and a half years before, when I first began planning this trip, I talked to Stan Stephens Cruises, a chartered boat tour company. They did not have a wheelchair-accessible boat then, but in the ad I had before me, there was a tiny wheelchair logo, indicating accessibility. I checked the time—11:30 p.m. central time. It was only 8:30 p.m. in Alaska. I called them immediately.

The chartered boat tour company had an eighty-five-foot cruise boat that is accessible by wheelchair. At that time of year, the boat took a 6.5-hour cruise in front of Columbia Glacier. Its waters were supposed to be teeming with puffins, harbor seals, Steller's sea lions, sea otters, whales, and many other critters. This is definitely a photographer's dream. I had thought that I was only going to be able to view the backside of this glacier from land. Since I had left a few days open in our itinerary, in case something came up, I immediately booked the tour for September 6, 2004.

The whole trip was miraculous, starting with what happened on the plane. The flight left from Chicago O'Hare and flew to Seattle, where, after a two-hour layover, we switched to Alaska

Airlines for the final flight to Juneau. Somehow, when we boarded the Alaska jet, my caregiver lost the carry-on bag with almost all my medical necessities in it, including diabetic testing equipment, syringes, and pills. Four flight attendants and my caregiver searched the entire plane, then held up the plane while they went back to search the terminal. The bag was nowhere to be found. We figured that it fell and somebody picked it up and walked off with it. The airline people asked if I wanted to continue on with the trip or return home. I said I was going on and that I would enjoy myself, even if it kills me. I figured I could replace the necessary supplies when we got to Haines. The plane finally took off. We landed in Ketchikan for arrivals and departures. Still no bag. We landed in Sitka for more arrivals and departures. Still no bag. We finally arrived in Juneau and deplaned—with no bag. The plane was scheduled to continue to Anchorage, and I figured that bag was gone forever.

Our hotel was across the street from the airport, and my caregiver was able to take a shuttle with the luggage. Since the shuttle was not wheelchair accessible, I just rolled the quarter mile to the hotel. Thirty minutes after we checked in, the phone rang. I figured it was my Haines contact, Dan Egolf, returning my call. I was going to ask him to contact the local health facility so I could replace my equipment, but it turned out to be the airport in Juneau. They had my bag! The flight attendants found it on the plane just before it took off for Anchorage. They had no idea where it had been.

What a relief!

The second miracle was the weather. The bald eagle festival was held the entire week before in Haines, and it had rained, sleeted, and snowed every day. It's always windy in the Chilkat Valley, but from the moment we arrived, we had flawless weather, high temperatures in the middle twenties, bright sunshine, and even in the valley—which runs north to south—there was not a breath of wind. After five days of intense photography, with only five hours per day of good light that time of year, I managed to shoot about 750 photographs, mostly of eagles.

All too soon, it was time to return home. Late the next evening, I called my newfound friends in Alaska to let them know we made it back safe and sound. We'd left Haines at 5:00 p.m. on Sunday evening, November 23. That night Haines was blanketed with twelve inches of snow. By Thursday—Thanksgiving—the town was buried under twenty-seven inches of snow. God wanted to show me that if you trust in Him everything turns out just right.

ONE-MAN SHOW

By January 2004, I had printed many of the photographs from the trip to the Chilkat Valley. One day, at my friends Andy and Nancy's house, we were discussing the plans for my upcoming dream trip, and I mentioned that I was toying with the idea of getting the new Nikon digital camera, which was due to be released in a few months. Because this camera would accept my Nikon lenses, all I had to buy was the camera body and a memory card. Still, this would cost a minimum of $1,300. I had the money saved for the trip, and I could get the new camera, but it would put a severe dent in my savings, and could I justify it to myself? I already had two Nikon cameras, a Nikon F3 and a Nikon 8008s. In truth, I think that I was actually more concerned about not wanting to make my darkroom obsolete by going digital.

After talking this over with me, Andy and Nancy said that they would pray about it. A few days later, Nancy said she had received an answer to her prayer. They would help me raise the money by putting on a showing of my new work at the Crystal Lake Holiday Inn, where Aglow International, a Christian women's organization, occasionally had their meetings. Nancy had the name of the contact person. I called her and was told that they would rent the meeting room for $100 for six hours. This seemed perfect. One hour to set it up, four hours for the show, and one hour to tear it down. I took the deal and we scheduled the show date for March 28, 2004.

With my friend Moy Siu Moy helping, we took three of the new Alaska photographs and pieced together a nice flyer that I could pass around and mail out; I also sent about 150 of these flyers by e-mail. When the date finally arrived, I was excited: this was to be my very first one-man show. The weather was not very good that day, with heavy rainstorms, but that didn't seem to matter. I was hoping to do well, but I never dreamed that I would do as well as I did. Up until then, the best I had ever done was at an Abilities Expo in Rosemont, a three-day show with one day to set up. It was a total of four days' work, and I did great—$1,250 in sales, almost twice what had previously been my best show.

When my one-man, four-hour show was over, Nancy totaled up the sales. If I had not been sitting in my chair, I think I would have hit the floor. God knew exactly what I needed because the camera body and a one gigabyte memory card cost $1,300. In that short four-hour show, with God's help, I did $1,400 in sales. I was dumbfounded. Praise the Lord!

That week, I went out and, without even thinking about making my darkroom obsolete, bought the new Nikon D70 digital camera, a one gigabyte memory card, an extra half-gigabyte memory card, an extra battery pack, and an extra three-year warranty—for a total of $1,600. I'm still practicing with the camera, and I love it; the photos are even sharper than I can get using my film cameras after I scan the images into the computer for printing.

Now—at least photographically speaking—I was ready for my dream trip. I planned on using all three cameras the whole time: the old Nikon F3 attached to the utility frame with a 1000 mm lens, the new Nikon digital camera mounted next to it on the utility frame with a 400 mm zoom lens and around my neck the Nikon 8008s with the 70 mm–300 mm zoom lens (or the 28 mm–90 mm zoom lens for any action shots that are not right in front of me). I can just swing up the 8008s with its auto focus function and, hopefully, get the shot, if I'm fast enough.

DREAM TRIP ALASKA

Since I began writing this book, and especially since my first Alaska adventure, I'd been thinking about the many trips I have taken in my life. In all those years, I cannot remember having even one day of weather bad enough to inhibit my going out to take photographs. (Snow doesn't bother me as much as rain, because rain and electric wheelchairs don't mix well.) Many long years before I admitted to myself that God even existed, He was watching over me. I don't claim to be the world's greatest photographer, and if I have not always gotten the shot, it's not because He didn't provide me with ample opportunity. Maybe God knew that my photography would one day glorify His creations so that people could see their beauty before man's greed destroys it all.

If I acted right and trusted in Him, I just knew I would have great weather and fantastic photo opportunities for my next Alaska trip. I prayed many times about whether or not this trip was something God wanted me to do. Since I was kind of new at this, I didn't always seem to hear His answers unless they hit me over the head.

I had been planning this trip in detail for two years, starting with inquiries to Denali Park lodges about accessibility and tour buses. I made reservations at the Brooks Lodge well over a year in advance. I thought I had every detail worked out. Now it was just a matter of waiting for September 1, 2004, to get here.

That Spring, I happened to be reading the book of Job. This was my second time reading this book of the Old Testament, but only the first since I had accepted Christ into my life as my personal Lord and Savior. When I was about midway through, everything about my perfectly planned trip started falling apart. First, the permit application to bring my rented van into Denali

National Park was denied. Then, when I called to confirm reservations at the Backcountry Lodge in Denali National Park, I was informed there had been a misunderstanding: the lodge was not accessible and their new tour buses were not equipped with wheelchair lifts. Right after that, I received an e-mail from Katmailand informing me that the large boat that the Quinnat Hotel was going to use to get me over to the Brooks Camp had not passed Coastguard inspection. They were prepared to give me a full refund, but I doubted that the airline would do the same.

The money, although substantial, was not the issue. A major part of my dream was to get to Katmai to photograph the Alaska brown bears fishing for salmon. I called the Quinnat and spoke to Todd, the manager, to get the whole story. The boat was falling apart due to the corrosive sea water and needed some major welding, but no master welder could be found in the town of King Salmon on the Aleutian Islands. The boat would have to be sent to Anchorage, repaired, and returned to King Salmon by barge, and this would take the whole season. I also found out that the viewing platforms at the Brooks Camp, although fully wheelchair accessible, have a four-foot high, almost solid railing around them, as does the boardwalk.

What else could possibly go wrong?

After talking with Todd, I realized that he had the weight of my chair wrong. He thought it was 700 pounds. I told him the chair weighs only 192 pounds and I weigh about 175 pounds, so together we are under 400 pounds. He said that that put everything in a new light. If I wanted to get over to the Brooks Camp badly enough, and if I was willing to work with him on it, we might be able to use the smaller boat, though it would be a rough trip. He said he would find a way to get me there and that I should call him back in a couple of weeks to see what he came up with.

Of course I wanted to call every day, but I waited. I decided to emulate Job: I was going to trust in the Lord. I praised the Lord every chance I got and refused to let myself become angry or fall into despair. I kept telling myself that this was a test of faith: if God wanted me to get there, He would get me there. I think this was the longest two weeks of my life.

When I called Todd again, he said they had located a master welder in a tiny town just fourteen miles from King Salmon and that they were trucking the boat there the next day; it would be fixed within a week. Days later, I received an e-mail from Denali National Park that my application for a disabled person's permit to bring my van into the park for one day had been approved. I discovered that the Denali Lodges also have cabins located just six miles south of the park entrance, one of which is ramped for wheelchairs. I booked that cabin for September 8–10, 2004 for the incredibly low price of $100 a night. (The Denali Wilderness Lodge would have been $285 per person per night.) The cabins have full facilities, with free access to two hot tubs you can enjoy after a hard day's hike or van ride.

Now that the problem of getting me to the Brooks Camp was solved, I still had to contend with the height of the solid railings around the viewing platforms. I was given the name of the person in charge at the Katmai National Park, Brooks Camp area. I explained my problem: I was not only short, but also confined to a short electric wheelchair. Instead of just dumping my problem in his lap, I suggested a simple solution. If they could possibly build me a portable four-by–four foot platform about one foot high with a three-foot ramp, this would bring the overall height of the railing down to three feet, which even I can see over. He told me it would be done and that they would move it anywhere I wanted on the three viewing platforms. Since this would be the first electric wheelchair at Brooks Camp that anyone could remember, they were intrigued.

Then I spoke with the engineer at Mr. Tool in Schaumburg, Ilinois, the tool-and-die shop that made my utility frame. He came up with an idea to make a temporary extension for the steering tiller of my wheelchair. If I sat on an extra cushion, I would gain an extra three to four inches of lift, making it easier to see over the forty-inch-high railings on the cruise boats.

With everything that had gone wrong, then all resolving itself when it seemed impossible, it showed me that, to the Lord, everything is a simple matter if you trust in Him.

By August 1, 2004, I was counting down the days—only one more month to go before I would leave on my dream trip, only now it was the dream trip of three people. Two young ladies were going with me and would assume the nursing, therapy, and caregiver duties. One of them, Bev Fisher, I have known almost since she was born. She is Murray and Carol Fisher's eldest daughter. At least I knew that no matter what happened, I would behave like a gentleman. That is, if I wanted to survive the trip.

Bev and her friend Jen Gil came during the third week in August so we could make the final preparations before we left. Not only did they learn all of my nursing and therapy care, they became familiar with the workings of this crazy electric wheelchair. Bev and Jen were as excited about this trip as I was, especially with the itinerary I had planned: seventeen days with twelve hours of daylight a day, and we were not planning to waste any of it.

This trip had been consuming almost my entire thought process for the last 2.5 years. I had not just been dreaming about it, but I was also reading every book about the birds, mammals, and even the road system in Alaska. I studied all the range maps for 375

different species of birds that are usually found there. Of all the birds, the ones I most wanted to photograph were the puffins, of which there are two species in Alaska—the tufted puffin and the horned puffin. According to the range maps, the tufted puffin is found commonly, in season, in the south coastal region. The horned puffin is found commonly, in season, in the southwest region, which only goes about as far east as Kodiak Island. I was thinking that I was only going to see one of the species, though one would be enough. One of the rangers of the Kenia Fjords National Park told me that both species are all over the Chiswell Islands, far out of the southwest range. Also when I booked the second trip into Prince William Sound to the Columbia Glacier at the eastern side of the sound, I was told that both puffin species are found there.

I had figured out that the birds don't pay any attention to range maps. I supposed that I would see whatever God wanted me to see, and not one species more or less, regardless of what our range maps said.

I'd gotten far too comfortable with the arrangements for the trip. Since everything went wrong back in March and April and then came back together again, I figured nothing could possibly go wrong now. I still prayed to the Lord, pretty much every day, but mostly to ask Him not to let anything go wrong. I forgot that I should be thanking Him each and every day even for the simplest things.

What happened to wake me up to the fact that I wasn't doing as well as I thought was an e-mail from Melissa, my contact at Katmailand:

Hi, David,

> We did get your payment, but unfortunately, the Quinnat Hotel called and said they will not have any boat going to Brooks for the rest of this year. Apparently they had big problems with their driver, who is no longer employed and have problems with both boats. I am very sorry about that. I have spoken to our manager in King Salmon and he says there is no way to guarantee we can get you and your wheelchair into any of our floatplanes. I'm not sure what we can do besides send a refund. You may want to call the Quinnat and speak to them yourself but I don't know what else they can tell you.

You can imagine what this did to me. A good portion of my dream involved getting to the Brooks Camp to photograph the great Alaskan coastal brown bear. Again I thought of the book of Job, and that was when I realized I had not been acting very thankful. I thanked the Lord for individual things that happened, but I forgot to thank Him for the things I take for granted every day, like waking up with a clear mind ready to face the new day or for the beautiful morning or for a good night's sleep or for just being there for me.

I called the Quinnat Hotel and spoke with the assistant manager, Tammy, and she explained what went wrong. It wasn't just the driver. The large boat blew an engine and the small boat had major problems too. After we talked and she realized how much this meant to me, she put me in touch with Tom, the owner of Katmai Air.

Tom told me they had a larger floatplane that could handle the job, though they couldn't guarantee there would not be a scheduling problem. They would pick me up and put me on the plane, they would also pick up my two-hundred-pound wheelchair and put it on the plane. After we landed, the whole process would be reversed, and they would carry me and my chair to the wheelchair-accessible trail. I was really thanking God now because everybody in Alaska was so willing to go to extremes to help me.

The next day, however, Katmai Air called and told me that after thinking about carrying my chair, me, Bev, and all my gear, they decided their plane couldn't handle it. Momentarily my dream crashed again, and I felt like the rug had been pulled out from under me. After letting my head clear, I again thought of the book of Job, and I prayed. Then I made two phone calls. The first was to Joel Ellis, head ranger at the Brooks Camp and of the entire Katmai National Park. I left a message explaining what had happened and asked if he had any suggestions. The second call was to Tammy at the Quinnat Hotel. After I explained my predicament to her, she agreed to make some calls to see if anyone else had a boat that could accommodate my chair and my party.

I tried not to worry. I kept telling myself that if it was God's will that I go, He would find some way of getting me there.

The very next day, I received a phone call from Northern Knights Wilderness Lodge. They had a twenty-eight-foot cabin cruiser and would be willing to transport my chair and party to and from the Brooks Camp for their standard fee of $600. This would entail lifting me from my wheelchair and carrying me into the boat; after getting me seated, they would carry my wheelchair onto the boat, but it would have to ride outside on the deck. That same day, I also received an e-mail from Joel Ellis. He had spoken with the people from Branch River Air at Bristol Bay, and they thought they could do the transport. I called them myself. After discussing all the problems and giving them the dimensions of the chair—its length, width and height—also its weight, my weight, Bev's approximate weight, and the weight of our gear, they said they could handle it all.

One nice thing was their price was even less expensive than the boat—$560 round trip. I had been on cabin cruisers many times in my life; the boat ride would be nothing new. And I had flown many times before—once in a small plane—but never in a floatplane. Taking off from and landing on the water would be an exciting new experience, and it would be faster, so I'd get a little more time to play with the bears.

With only fifteen days left until departure, I prayed no other mishaps came up. I also remembered to thank the Lord for everything—and I mean *everything*—all the time.

DREAM TRIP TO ALASKA

September 1 finally arrived. I couldn't imagine waiting one day longer. The suitcases, my camera equipment, and my medical supplies were packed, checked and double-checked. My friend Jim came at dawn to drive Bev, her friend Jen, and me to the airport in my van. We would be flying into Anchorage, then driving a rented van south to the town of Seward on the Kenia Peninsula.

The most important thing I had planned for this first portion of the trip was the 10.5 hour boat tour into the Kenia Fjords, traveling up to the Northwestern Fjord, where I hoped to photograph puffins, mures, other sea birds, and—God willing—whales, Orcas, and other sea creatures. The next day, we would take a 4.5 hour trip from Whittier, just north of Seward, into Prince William Sound to photograph glaciers. We would spend part of a day at the Exit Glacier, a smaller slightly inland glacier that you can hike up to. From the Kenia Peninsula we would travel by van all the way to Valdez on the other side of Prince William Sound for a boat tour of the Columbia Glacier, where I hoped for more puffins, whales and any other sea life. From Valdez we would drive back west and north to Denali National Park and spend three days there. The highlight of the whole trip would be our last three days at Brooks Camp in Katmai National Park, which we would get to by flying from Anchorage to King Salmon, and then from King Salmon to Brook's camp by floatplane. This is where I would get my best chance to photograph the great coastal Alaska brown bear up close in the wild.

Before taking off from Chicago, I had a chance to ask the pilot if we would fly towards Seattle and turn northwest over the Gulf of Alaska, or would we fly as the crow flies, which would take us over the southwest tip of Canada? It turned out we would head northwest until we were over Fargo, North Dakota, then north into Canadian airspace until we were just over the edge of Hudson Bay.

Through the scattered clouds I was able to catch glimpses of land often enough to enjoy the sights. As we crossed the Canadian Rockies, the sky cleared and I looked down on those giant peaks covered with glaciated areas of centuries-old packed ice. All I could think to do was thank the Lord for such unparalleled beauty. The plane banked over Hudson Bay, but we were too high to see if there were any polar bears gathering on the shores. They would be waiting for the waters to freeze so they could move out onto the ice for the winter. I didn't really expect to see any polar bears; that was another dream for another time, if the Lord directed me there.

The six-hour non-stop flight went quickly. We landed in Anchorage without delay, although I waited half an hour for them to get me off the plane. After I was reunited with my wheelchair, we retrieved our luggage and met up with Bev's friend Jen, who had flown in a few days before. Next we located our rental van, loaded our stuff into it, and hopped onto the Seward Highway.

Even before we cleared the city limits, the sights were fantastic—towering glacier-capped mountains in every direction!—but the sky was overcast and raining lightly, and I was a little disappointed and grumpy. Milepost Magazine gives you all the available pullouts and points of interest along the road by mile marker number, but we saw no mile markers, and so we missed the first scenic point I wanted to photograph, The Chapel by the Sea. We got to Potters Marsh but, because of the rain, I didn't get my utility frame hooked up. There were a few ducks and terns around, but nothing close enough for me to identify or photograph. Continuing south, we stopped at almost all the pullouts just to look at the changing scenes. I took many photographs and wondered what these same scenes would look like if the weather had been clear.

We made it down to Seward about seven in the evening, checked into the Windsong Lodge, and dined on grilled fresh Alaska salmon, which even Bev and Jen, both vegetarians, enjoyed. The next day was still overcast, but luckily, the rain was down to a drizzle. We had planned a day-long boat tour into the Kenia Fjords National Park, but at the marine operations office, we were met with discouraging news. Because of windy conditions outside Resurrection Bay, the tour might be cancelled. We had a choice of not going and getting a full refund of $165 each, or taking the chance of going and, if the tour was cancelled, getting a partial refund. For me at least, there was no choice; I wanted to photograph the Kenia Fjords and all its wildlife. There was no way to reschedule. In thinking that the Lord would grant me perfect weather every day, I'd left no extra time to use as backup.

The protected waters of Resurrection Bay seemed calm enough, but as we neared the southern end of the bay, even I had to admit that the waters were getting more than a little rough. The captain announced the tour would have to be cancelled. He had received an SOS call from another tour boat that had blown a seal gasket on an engine. We maneuvered into position in the rough waters to tie up with the disabled boat so that the passengers could board our boat. Then we made our way back to Fox Island. It was very windy but at least the rain had stopped, and in those moments when the boat quit bobbing, I was able to get some great photos of the surrounding mountains meeting the waters.

At Fox Island, everyone hiked to the lodge for a baked salmon lunch. I stayed on the boat because it was peaceful and easier; my lunch was brought to me. I'm afraid I didn't do too well in praising the Lord in the face of the great disappointment at not getting to see the Kenia Fjords, which meant no puffin photographs and almost no sea life. I did thank Him for the intense beauty that was all around us, but I couldn't understand why the weather was not with us. I was wondering if I had done something wrong and if this was some kind of punishment.

On our way back to Seward, the captain got as near as he could in the rough waters to a sea lion haulout. There were over a dozen Steller's sea lions, and I got some good photos, though I expected many of them were blurry because of the moving boat. After we left the haulout area, the captain spotted a few sea otters and brought the boat close. From my vantage point on the back deck, the only wheelchair-accessible area on the boat, I was able to get a couple of photos, but I knew they wouldn't be very good. Darn boat just wouldn't quit rocking. We also saw a couple of puffins in the water, but between the rocking boat and the bobbing puffins, I didn't get any photos of them either; it would have been difficult for even an able-bodied photographer with two good arms and two good legs. Now the only hope I had to get puffin shots was in a few days, when we would take the 6.5 hour tour to the Columbia Glacier out of Valdez.

That night I cleaned the saltwater spray off the camera lenses, downloaded the digital photos to a CD and stored it away for safekeeping. Then I prayed for better weather.

The weather was clearer over the next few days. On the drive to Whittier, we caught glimpses of Portage Glacier, a beautiful sight, especially early in the morning. Everything looked different from when we drove through the area only two days earlier under cloudy skies and light rain. Though there was fog in the low areas—giving the whole scene a spooky look—it was beautiful, and I was elated at having such a perfect day for this side trip.

To get to Whittier from the Seward Highway, you go through a long one-lane tunnel and pay a toll of $12. The tunnel going into Whittier is open for fifteen minutes on the half hour, fifteen minutes on the hour going away from Whittier; the rest of the time only trains can pass. A unique and interesting system! After we paid our toll, we sat in the ten-lane staging area and waited for a stoplight to tell us when to proceed. With our headlights on, we drove through at 25 miles per hour. Though it's only about a mile, it felt like much longer. Soon enough, we began to see the light at the end of the tunnel—no pun intended—and emerged into a picturesque valley on the western end of Prince William Sound, its calm blue waters surrounded by mountains and waterfalls.

At the boat tour office, we got in line with the forty or so other people waiting to board, then proceeded down the long pier. The eighty-five-foot long tour boat was basically the same as the one used for the Kenia Fjords tours. The only outside area accessible to me was on the back deck, but I had the whole width of the boat, about twelve by seven feet. A few obstacles made maneuvering difficult—davits in the floor for mooring the support poles, plus a ladder going to the upper deck. Luckily, the captain was aware of me and tried to maneuver the boat so that I could get some clear shots from the side of the back deck. Some able-bodied people were not as considerate. They seemed to be ignorant of the fact that I wasn't able to move around as freely as they. Even though they could stand and take photographs from two other decks, they seemed to gravitate to a spot directly in my line of vision. I was, however, able to control my temper.

Pulling away from the pier in Whittier Harbor, we headed across the small bay toward a beautiful large waterfall pouring down the cliff side into the sound. As we got nearer, we saw that the whole cliff was a massive kittiwake rookery. Kittiwakes are gull-like birds. I got some good photos of them and the waterfall.

Then the captain announced that there were some young bald eagles up ahead. He got close enough for me to photograph two fledglings standing on a rock right at the water's edge. The parents were above, raising a ruckus with the kittiwakes. What a great way to start a boat tour!

We moved out of the harbor towards the open waters of the sound, along the peninsula of land where Whittier is situated. When we reached the end, we doubled back on the opposite side and headed west into Blackstone Bay toward Blackstone Glacier. Multiple glaciers make up this small region, and it is unbelievably beautiful, especially today. As we neared the glaciers we saw that the surrounding mountainsides were dotted with waterfalls pouring down into Blackstone Bay. Breathtaking!

Soon, a sudden fierce windstorm, a williwaw, shrieked in off the ocean. I had to cover my cameras with plastic bags against the spray from the high waves. We headed back in rough waters. It was difficult for the captain to control the boat, but we reached Whittier Harbor without mishap, and though we were a little behind schedule, we still made it through the 6:00 p.m. tunnel opening. The drive back down to Seward was peaceful. While Bev and Jen rested at the hotel, I roamed Exit Glacier Road with my camera. It was still bright and sunny, though windy now. Not far from the lodge I encountered a black squirrel looking around for something to eat. Then I saw a couple of gulls flying over the river. At last, something alive and moving!

From the hotel, it was only an eleven-mile drive to Exit Glacier, a once-massive glacier that has receded about 150 yards over the last half century. There is a partially paved trail that leads up to the glacier face, not an easy trail because once the pavement ends, you are basically on the bare ground where the glacier once stood, rutted with many shallow ravines and many, many rocks of various sizes. It took me quite a while to get there, but it was worth it. Despite having receded so much, the glacier is still a massive chunk of flowing ice with a crevassed face about fifteen to twenty feet thick. We explored all morning then started the drive north to Eagle River.

On the way, we stopped at a small resort named Aleskya, which had an enclosed ski tram lift that was wheelchair accessible. I figured it would be nice to ride to the top and get some photos. The 2,200-foot ride took only four minutes. I had been thinking I would be seeing the mountains the way they were from the plane, forgetting that 2,200 feet is not so high when the surrounding mountains are ten to twelve thousand feet—my mistake, but it was still a very nice view from up top.

At the camera store in Anchorage, Jen returned the digital camera she had purchased and got the next better model. We inquired about a large park where, I had been told, moose are frequently seen. The park borders the Air Force base and Cook's Inlet and is open to the public. A ranger suggested that the best way to spot moose is simply to drive slowly through the park while keeping our eyes open. Five minutes later, we encountered another car that had stopped for a young bull moose that was standing along the roadside. About fifteen feet past the bull moose was a cow with a good -sized calf. I got out of the van quickly and started shooting pictures, but the bull was not going to cooperate. He crossed the road, then wandered off into the brush. The cow and calf were much more cooperative, and I got some good photos.

In the meantime, the bull had doubled back across the road and found a nice spot for a rest, right across a path where some poor guy had gotten off the bicycle for a look. The bull moose had lain down about six feet away from the bicycle. Since you do not want to wake up a resting bull moose just to get your bicycle back, the guy waited with the rest of us until the moose awoke on his own and moved off. Now that we had seen a little wildlife, I felt much more optimistic.

The next day was blessedly clear again, perfect for a little 285-mile drive along the base of the Chugatch Mountains, then down through the Keystone Canyon to Valdez. A great deal of the area we passed through at the base of the mountains was glaciated. At every curve in the road, we were treated to a new vista, tall rugged mountains with jagged peaks, sometimes with towering cliffs, sometimes a deep valley, and always lush deep green evergreen forests growing right up to the edge of the glaciers, streams, and waterfalls at every turn.

The only thing that could make me happier was sighting wildlife. In TV specials on Alaska, moose, elk, caribou, and bears were everywhere along the roads. That is the Alaska I dreamed about, and what I was expecting to see. With three of us on the lookout, I thought we would spot a great deal of wildlife. We didn't. By this time, and after talking with some local people, I realized that the Alaska of my dreams was thirty-six years old. Civilization had moved in, bringing with it people, traffic and, unfortunately, hunters—the kind who hunt with a high-powered rifle instead of a camera. Also, September is already the start of the winter season up here, and many of the migratory animals were already on the move.

We finally reached the town of Glenallen, where we picked up Highway 4 to Valdez. This area is even more glaciated and there are at least three good-sized waterfalls right next to the road. Unfortunately, only two of these falls have pull-offs where we could park the car to take photographs. One is Horsetail Falls and the other is Bridal Veil Falls, half a mile away.

After dinner in Valdez, we backtracked out of town to the road that leads to the old Valdez Cemetery along the eastern edge of the bay. This is where, we were told, a grizzly sow and her cubs had been coming regularly to fish in the shallow waters of the bay. We didn't see any bears, but there were a few hawks and a whole lot of gulls; it was also a great place to catch a beautiful, peaceful sunset. Bev and I went back up the road the next morning to photograph the waterfalls, but there was a slight miscalculation on my part. The sunlight doesn't reach inside the canyon in the area of the falls until at least midafternoon, so it was both very dark and darn cold. Not only that, I left my utility frame at the hotel. I tried to hold the camera in my hand. No luck: it was much too dark, and my hand felt frozen.

On the bright side, it was a perfect day for the long boat trip we would be taking to the Columbia Glacier—clear, beautiful blue sky with calm waters. We walked over to the dock from the hotel.

Once we got settled on the boat, I explained to one of the crew that I was working on just one and a half lungs; my right lung is still partly collapsed from the accident. Also, I hate the stench of cigarette smoke, and I was limited to the back deck—which is normally the smoking area. I told him that if anybody lit up near me, they would be going swimming. (I try to be diplomatic, but smoking is something that really gets to me.) An announcement was made over the intercom that if anyone wanted to smoke, they should see a crew person and arrangements would be made elsewhere.

As we headed west out of Valdez harbor, we saw the backside of the majestic Chugatch Mountains to the north; behind us to the east were more mountains; to the south, more mountains. The cabin blocked my forward view, but I knew that beyond the open waters, there were more mountains far to the west. Before we even left the harbor, the captain announced that sea otters were ahead. He circled around so everybody could see the small groups of otters floating on their backs in a kelp bed, just enjoying the weather. I got about twenty good photos. It was a pretty great way to start a cruise and made up for the one slightly sour note I encountered right off the bat— people trying to crowd in front of me. Again and again I had to ask a certain couple to move so that I could get some photographs. I missed more than a few because I was trying to be polite and calm and not scream at them.

Ninety minutes later, we saw our first iceberg, but the boat just sped past. I started to get angry, wondering why the captain didn't slow down, not realizing that this was just the first of thousands of beautiful icebergs that appeared as we drew closer to Columbia Glacier.

The captain steered near a sea lion haulout, but there were no sea lions. We saw a few puffins in the water, but because there were always people crowded in front of me, I was unable to get any photos. Also, with the boat going in one direction and the puffins swimming in the opposite direction, I had only seconds to maneuver and shoot. I had been using the tiller extension that Mr. Tool made for me, plus the four-inch spacer cushion. That extra four inches made a whole lot of difference, especially when you are short and dealing with forty-two-inch railings.

Nearing Columbia Glacier, icebergs of all shapes and sizes were everywhere, so if somebody got in front of me, I simply turned and shot another one. For a while, I was shooting from the back of the boat, and the only way anyone could squeeze in front of me would be to balance on the railing and risk a very cold bath.

Columbia Glacier is continually calving off huge chunks of ice—some as big as a large building—and causing huge waves. For this reason, the boat kept its distance at about a third of a mile, but it was close enough to see everything. The face of the glacier is about two hundred feet high and a good half mile wide, an unbelievably magnificent hunk of flowing ice with shimmering hues of blue set against a backdrop of towering mountains and a perfect blue sky.

The captain tried other spots for sea lions, but no luck. We saw more puffins on the way back, but I had no luck photographing them. Soon we came to the most beautiful waterfall I'd ever seen, the water shooting out of the mountain at least ten feet before plummeting to the waters a good hundred feet below. In a nearby pine tree were two bald eagles, but I could not even get a good look because this same annoying couple, whom I had asked repeatedly not to stand in front of me, was crowding in front of me again. The man turned to me and asked if I got a good shot of the eagles. That was when I blew my stack. "You have an eighty-five-foot boat with two decks that you can go on," I yelled. "I have about six feet of space to do my work in. Why do you insist on crowding in front of me? Go somewhere else!" I didn't see them the rest of the trip. I have quite a few shots of beautiful icebergs with this man's elbow in the photo. Thank God for digital cameras and Photoshop.

As we neared the harbor, there was a large buoy anchored in the water with four Steller's sea lions sunning themselves on it. I got some goofy photos with no elbows in them. Praise the Lord! I'd taken just over three hundred photos on this boat tour of some of the most beautiful scenery I had ever seen.

Every resident I talked to said that if you can make it past the first year in Alaska, you will never leave. Nobody takes the mountains for granted because they are always changing, nor can you predict what might be around the next bend in the road. We took one on the way to Wasilla and were treated to another new sight—a young moose, already about the size of a large horse, standing on a grassy knoll beside the road.

The next day was the anniversary of my accident. September 8, 1981—not a day I liked to think about. I still found it hard to believe I'd spent the last twenty-three years in this chair. I know I never would have made it this far without Sue, and I wished that she were here with me now to enjoy all this beauty.

Once, over a dozen years ago, I had been joking with her about my upcoming anniversary all week long. But when the date came, busy in my darkroom, I managed temporarily to forget about it, though I was somewhat depressed all day. That evening, when Sue tried to do therapy on my arm, I couldn't even tolerate it. I didn't know what was wrong; I just felt so down. Alone in my dining room in the semidarkness, looking up at a wall covered with owl photos, I realized there were tears flowing out of my eyes. I couldn't stop them. Then I remembered the date.

For the first ten or so years after the accident, I tended to react this same way whenever we drove past the intersection where the accident happened. Retrograde amnesia had kept the trauma hidden from the conscious part of me for all those years, but my subconscious remembered, and my eyes would fill with tears.

I hoped that this year would be different. Today I would be going to Denali National Park. When I mapped out the itinerary for this trip, I hadn't even thought about where I would be on the anniversary date, and originally, I had made other plans. But I could see now that it would work out perfectly. What better place in the world could there be for me to spend this anniversary day than a place I had dreamed of most of my adult life?

At breakfast in the hotel, I struck up a conversation with a couple from Utah who had just returned from Denali. Of course, I had to ask what kind of critters they encountered. They said they had seen quite a few bears up close, as well as a few caribou, some Dall sheep, and a moose in the distance.

As we drove up to Denali, I prayed for a clear day, and my prayers were granted. After a while, we came to a sign that announced a pull-off from which to view Mount McKinley—known as *Denali* in the native language—which was 107 miles away. I was totally amazed to be able to see it so clearly from that distance, this huge, almost-white mountain surrounded by a much smaller and darker Alaskan mountain range. I thanked God for this day and started taking photos, first of the mountain, then of Bev with Denali in the background, then of Jen with Denali. Then I gave the camera to Bev and asked her to get a couple of shots of me with Denali in the background. *Denali* means "the great one," and the mountain really lives up to its name.

I was dismayed that there had been absolutely no wildlife in any field or stream that we passed. Again I prayed for this to change. When we arrived at Denali later that morning, we were allowed to drive our own vehicle into the park for the first sixteen miles; beyond that, we needed a special permit, else we can hike or ride a tour bus. We found the park ranger's office, checked in, and picked up the special one-day permit we had been granted. We were required to watch a twenty-five minute video on the rules of the road in the park.

The weather was still perfect: We were being treated to only the fifth completely clear day of the year. Because of its great elevation, Denali is clouded over much of the time, and the raging wildfires that were still burning northwest of Fairbanks added smoke to the normal cloudiness. The whole park is magnificent, with deep-green evergreen forests, many rivers, small lakes and ponds, and beautiful foliage everywhere. We drove in as far as we were allowed, then parked in a small area to get out and look around. Fantastic rock outcroppings everywhere. Sunlight reflecting off the river in the valley made it look like a ribbon of silver. Signs cautioned us to watch out for moose the next five miles, but we saw no moose. We explored for a few hours, and though I was limited as to where I could go—there are no wheelchair-accessible trails in this beautiful wilderness area—Bev and Jen were able to hike around.

Later, we drove into Hub, a tiny tourist town of mostly restaurants and gift shops right outside the park. We had dinner and picked up some lunch—from a Subway Sandwich Shop, of all places—for the next day's bus tour.

Back at the cabins, a driver who worked for Denali Lodges told me he had just seen a moose cow with two calves about a half mile up the road. That was all I needed to hear! I grabbed my camera, and off I went. As soon as I caught up with them, the moose and calves crossed the road. Cars were stopped in both directions, everyone watching or taking pictures. I just sat on the side of the road, and the female walked to within twenty feet of me. Even in the fading light, I could see how beautiful she was.

I felt blessed by that day. This was one anniversary I would never forget. Not only had I realized my dream of getting to Denali National Park, but the Lord granted me perfect weather so that I could fully enjoy the splendor of this magnificent place.

The tour bus we rode in the next day was a converted school bus whose windows open down from the top. This was fine for an able-bodied person who could kneel on the seat to aim a camera out the open window. For someone in a wheelchair, it was impossible. You cannot even get close to a window you can open. Plus, the open part of the window was well above my head. The bus stopped for wildlife viewing, but for safety reasons, passengers are allowed off only at scenic overlooks.

I had figured that, for wildlife photography, this trip would be a waste of time. I would get the lay of the land and take pictures of the scenery. The area for wheelchairs was in the rear of the bus on the driver's side, where seats had been removed and a lift installed. The drivers are supposed to lock down the wheelchairs using a belt arrangement. That wasn't good for me. I can barely move my head to the left and cannot see much on that side. I convinced the driver not to lock down my chair. This way, I would be able to sit at an angle holding on to the lift so that I could look in both directions by just by moving my chair a little.

Shortly into the tour we saw some ptarmigan, large grouse-like birds native to the extreme northwest. They turn completely white in the winter, and these beautiful individuals were half white already. Of course, I could only sit and look out the window and try not to get too frustrated because I could not capture this beauty on camera. Not long afterward, we spotted our first Alaska brown bear (a larger cousin to the grizzly of the lower forty-eight), and I grew even more frustrated. After that we saw many grizzlies. I managed to get a few pictures by waiting until no one was sitting near the open window in the last seat of the bus and the bears were far up on a hillside, where I could shoot at an upwards angle.

We stopped at the Eilson pull off the main scenic photographic point for viewing Mount McKinley. This vantage point really takes your breath away. On this crystal-clear day, the third in a row, we could see all the way to the very top of the mountain. I felt really blessed.

We continued to Kantishna, with me holding on to the lift. On the way back, about seven hours into the trip, I dozed off briefly, and of course, this was just when the driver had to make a hairpin turn to stay on the winding mountain road. He hit a bump, and I woke up to feel my chair tipping to the left. Unable to catch myself in time, I jammed my head and neck badly, but the worst part was my brand new 80–400 mm autofocus zoom lens had taken a good whack, and I couldn't use it. Thank God I had also brought my 300 mm zoom lens. I assured the driver I was all right. We made it back to the visitors' center without further mishap, but I didn't doze off again—that's for sure.

Later I discovered that the camera worked fine; I just had to make do without the 400 mm zoom lens. I thanked God that I still had the use of the digital camera and the 300 mm lens. I got very little sleep because my neck was in agony, and I was more than a little worried.

I woke early the next morning from a painful slumber. After Bev and I did the usual therapy to loosen up my legs, I asked her to hold onto the sides of my head and pull gently while I turned my head back and forth. This slight disarticulation allowed the neck vertebrae to realign themselves and relieved the pain and stiffness quite a bit. My neck still hurt, but at least now I could move it a little.

Today we would use the disabled person permit and drive our rented van into the park, and I would finally be able to get some photos of wildlife. I was excited to be free of the bus and moving on our own. Not long after we passed the sixteen-mile checkpoint, driving at the posted 25 mile per hour, I called to Bev to stop. There was a covey of ptarmigan by the roadside. Bev and Jen got the ramps out quickly, and I was able to photograph these birds from as close as eight or nine feet. About an hour later, we spotted our first two grizzlies about two hundred yards off the road. I took some photos out the open door of the van, but the bears were a little too far away for a good photo with a 300 mm lens. In a while we spotted another pair of grizzlies, this time only about fifty yards away; I got some good shots from inside the van with the side doors open.

On our way back, we came up behind a line of vehicles watching and photographing grizzlies. We were slowly moving along, looking for a spot that was safe to offload me, when we saw a fox trotting towards us, a beautiful gray-and-red mix who was determined to stay on the road. I couldn't get a photo, but Bev put the van in reverse and backed up so that we could stay abreast of him. Jen managed to get a shot or two out the window. When the fox disappeared into the brush, I got out and went bear hunting with my camera. I got some shots of one before it went down into a gully—and that was the end of that. But I was having a great time. Finally, this was the Alaska I'd dreamed of all these years!

On our return to the east-end checkpoint, we spotted another bear about fifty feet from the road. We stopped and got the side doors open. This bear looked hungry, so we kept a close eye on him as he walked toward the van. About twenty-five feet away, he decided to lean over and scratch his back on a short scrub tree; then he rolled over. Nothing is cuter than a cuddly teddy bear squirming on its back with all four feet sticking up in the air. He sat up and looked around to see who was watching. A tour bus pulled up. The bear crossed the road and went through the whole routine again. His angle to the van wasn't good, so I got only a few photos, but that was okay because I enjoyed watching him.

About a mile up and only two miles from the east-end check point, Bev spotted something up on a hillside. At first I thought it was another bear, but it was a magnificent bull moose, the largest I'd ever seen. If Bev and Jen hadn't gotten the ramps out so quickly, I probably would have flown out the side of the van—I was that excited! With tears of joy in my eyes, all I could say is, "Thank you, Lord. Thank you!"

I took shot after shot. The moose had his head down, grazing on a small ridge covered in foliage that was already ablaze in fall colors. I kept talking to the tiny moose in my viewfinder on the camera, and every time I said, "Come on, raise your head," his head went up. Each time he returned to his grazing, I said, "Look this way," and he did. This went on for nearly half an hour. Then he started to move away, and I said, "No, come this way. Come closer." That's when he turned and headed along the ridge, toward the road. Wonderful! Every few feet, he stopped to look around. I kept praising the Lord. I asked Bev how she spotted him, and she said she saw sunlight glinting off his antlers. It was six in the evening. We were facing east, and he was east of us, the sun to our backs. He was a perfect specimen in a perfect photo opportunity.

I kept saying, "Thank you, Lord. He is magnificent." I said this over and over, I couldn't stop.

The moose kept walking, grazing, pausing to look at me, until he was only about one hundred feet away on top of the small ridge, perfectly outlined against the clear blue sky. At this point, after shooting off a few more photos, I decided it would be prudent to return to the van. It was rutting season, and moose have been known to charge.

By this time a tour bus had pulled up beside our van, and everybody was taking photos from the windows. Believing that Bev was behind me, I started up the ramps—only to realize too late that she wasn't there. I got about a third of the way up the ramps before I flipped over backward. My mind was clear, as if I was falling in slow motion. I thought that I'd better save the camera, and I put my hand up to keep it from crashing to the ground.

There I was, lying on my back, strapped into my chair with my legs sticking up in the air—a little like that cute grizzly. Three men rushed from the tour bus to help me right myself. After they got me into the van and I thanked them, I started to laugh. I think I was so elated by this moose-shooting opportunity I could have fallen down the mountainside and not felt a thing. Then I realized something that made me laugh even harder. The intense pain I had in my neck all last night and all day was completely gone. Whatever I had jammed in my neck the day before by falling over sideways, I evidently unjammed by falling over backward. (I do not recommend you try this at home unless you are a professional stuntman.)

I thanked the Lord for this completely remarkable day and for His healing chiropractic touch. I took 130 photographs of that moose—the most amazing moose I have ever seen—and all but a few turned out to be excellent, full of vibrant fall colors and pure blue sky. Some people will scoff, but I think this moose was a direct gift from the Lord. Maybe He holds some things back so that when He finally reveals them, they will make an even bigger impression. When I was finally able to fall asleep, I slept restfully and at complete peace, knowing in my heart that the Lord was with me.

September 11 dawned with a kind of finality because we were leaving Denali. Would I ever be able to return? Only the Lord knows that. If He wants me to come back here, I sure wouldn't argue with Him.

We picked up a hitchhiker, a young tourist from the Czech Republic. I asked if he enjoyed Alaska; he replied that he had and that it was very beautiful. Conversation was limited because my hearing in a moving vehicle is terrible and his English was heavily accented and broken. Anyway, he soon fell asleep. We dropped him off when we got to Anchorage. At dinner that night, we said good-bye to Jen. In the morning, Bev and I would catch a flight to King Salmon at the base of the Aleutian Islands, while Jen, who could not afford the next—and most expensive—leg of the journey, would return home.

We waited—and waited—for the wheelchair-accessible taxi to pick us up for the two-mile drive to the airport the next morning. Whenever I have flown, I'd just roll to the door of the plane on the extending walkway from the terminal where they'd transfer me to the aisle chair to get me to my seat on the plane; at the other end of the flight, the procedure is reversed. This was how it was done at the Anchorage airport when we arrived from Chicago on the full-sized jet. Now, though, we were flying to King Salmon on a much smaller Alaska Airlines jet. This is where things would be getting interesting.

Once Bev and I cleared the security check, we were directed to our gate, and when it was time to board, we were taken to a service elevator and down to the tarmac level. From there, I rolled out to where the plane was sitting. Now they transferred me into the aisle chair, which was then wheeled onto a DPL (disabled person lifter)—basically a small boxcar on a large forklift. This device is also used to load food services onto the plane. The boxcar was raised to the height of the plane door, and I was wheeled in and transferred into my seat for the fifty-eight-minute flight.

King Salmon is a small airport, far away from any big cities. They don't even have the use of a DPL. This time, the airline people got me out first, transferring me to the aisle seat and then carrying me down the long flight of steep, narrow stairs to the tarmac. My chair was waiting, and they transferred me into it. I was more than a little tense when they were carrying me down that long flight of steps because one slip would have been more than just painful, but the entire experience was exciting. It was a little difficult for the airline people who have to do the carrying because, at about 175 pounds, I'm no lightweight.

The people at the Quinnat Hotel really went out of their way to help us. They removed the middle seat from the van and rigged-up ramps for me. They talked to the Branch River Air people to coordinate tomorrow's thirty-minute floatplane flight to the Brooks Camp. We arrived at the hotel in midafternoon, and their restaurant was closed, so they offered to pick up our dinner from a restaurant in town. We placed our order and told them what time we wanted to eat. After chatting a while with the people I'd been in communication with over the Internet and on the phone for the past months, I went out with my camera to look around. When I returned around five, Todd, the hotel's general manager, got our dinners—delicious grilled halibut—after which I went outside to photograph the spectacular sunset.

The next day, we had perfect weather to do something I never dreamed I would do—fly in a floatplane. I never thought they could get me into one.

Hoping to get my first close view of the Alaska coastal brown bear in the wild, I was in the lobby long before it was time to leave, rolling back and forth (my rendition of pacing). It was a short ride to Branch River Air. Dave Wagner, the pilot, guided my chair down a long steep ramp to their pier, where the Cessna 206 Stationaire was tied down. After some discussion about the best way to do this, they transferred me to a regular kitchen chair they brought, dismantled my Braun Triwheeler and stowed the chair in the floatplane. Then they picked me up in a fireman's carry—two men each taking one arm and one leg—maneuvered onto the float and from there stepped up onto a rung, all without dropping me into the water. They hoisted me into the plane to a seat on the floor, got me as comfortable as possible, put a floatation life vest on me, and strapped me in. After Dave ran through the safety routine a few times, Bev climbed on board.

It was noisy as we taxied away from the pier, and I couldn't see very well from my seat on the floor, but I held my autofocus camera up to the window. It was only a thirty-minute, sometimes very bumpy flight—lots of potholes up here—but it was great. We landed on the water and taxied as close to the rocky shore as possible. Joel Ellis, the head ranger at Katmai National Park, was waiting with some other rangers. After getting me unloaded—again without dropping me into the lake—they carried me to a gator truck, a small open truck used to transport people and gear from the floatplanes to the lodge. While I waited and they unloaded our gear and my heavy chair and packed that into another gator truck, I watched other floatplanes landing on and taking of from this lake. About two hundred yards away, I saw a female bear (a sow) and her three cubs fishing from the shore—a beautiful first sight for me!

For the two-mile drive to Brooks Camp Lodge, Joel drove the truck with the gear; the other ranger, Imes, drove the truck Bev and I were in. Along the way, Imes pointed out the turnoff trail that leads to the falls and riffles observation platforms. We continued on for another mile to the lower platform area. All three of these platforms are beautifully ramped and completely accessible.

We stopped for a few minutes, and I couldn't believe my eyes. I never imagined it would be anything like this. Television specials concentrate on the falls and riffles platform in July, when the biggest salmon are jumping; they never show the lower platform area. Like a special greeting from the Lord, there were eighteen bears—boars, sows and cubs—visible in this small area near the platform. I had thought that the Alaska Brown Bears in Denali National Park were big, but these coastal Alaska brown bears were huge, almost a full 30 percent larger.

We crossed the Brooks River on a floating bridge and followed the trail on the other side. It runs for a while alongside the river, about seven or eight feet from the water, and now there were huge bears just twenty or thirty feet away. Two young boars (males) were play-fighting in the water about thirty feet offshore. Imes stopped the truck long enough for me to snap off about six shots using the 300 mm zoom lens set at 200 mm. At this magnification, on a sunny day, I can hand hold the camera steadily enough for good photos.

Farther up, at an area called the point, the trail turns away from the river for some fifty yards, then turns parallel to the river again and continues for another 150 yards or so to the lodge and cabins. We stopped in an open area outside the dining hall. First they unloaded and assembled my wheelchair, then they unloaded me and got me seated correctly in the chair. Finally they unloaded everything else and carried it into the cabin.

Now we had to go to bear school and watch a thirty-minute video about the dos and don'ts of bear viewing in the wild. When hiking on the trails, you should talk or make some kind of noise to let the bears know you are there. You do not want to surprise a one-thousand-pound bear. You must stay a minimum of fifty yards away from a boar and one hundred yards away from a sow with cubs. These bears can move as fast as 40 miles per hour. You should not carry any kind of food in your pockets. Should you encounter a bear up close, do not run: their prey runs. Just talk gently or make some noise and back away slowly. These encounters are few and far between because there are rangers all over the place in radio contact with one another, telling each other where a bear has been seen, and frequently trails are closed because of bears sleeping on them.

I sat patiently through bear school and lunch after, and then I could wait no longer to get hooked up in my utility frame. With my digital camera fitted with the 300 mm lens, I took off for the lower platform. I waited with a few people at the Point because a bear was close to the cedar bridge—they like to chew on the wood—but we were soon allowed to cross. The ranger stayed with me and told me to keep moving because they didn't want anyone to stop on the bridge while the bears were so close. We got across easily, and I was shown which ramp to take to get onto the lower platform. Actually, there were two platforms connected by a walkway, and I could get to either one.

The ramps and the bridge had gates across them to keep bears off, so I needed help whenever I wanted to cross the bridge or go onto a platform. I was happy to see the four-by-four-foot elevated platform they added on the lower platform to help me photograph over the railings.

This was what dreams are made of. I was having a great time, and time was flying by. Soon it was time for dinner. Meals are served buffet style at set hours, and most of the other people viewing the bears had left. I was trapped on the platform by a sow (who was designated by the number 410) and her three cubs. They were napping on the trail between the bridge and the Point.

I overheard another tourist talking to the ranger about going to the falls platform. When I asked if I could join him, he said, "Sure."

We chatted as we went along the trail, and I discovered he was with a film crew from Virginia, and they were there to film the Brooks Camp area for a television program called *Campgrounds of America*. Every so often, he called out, "Hey, bear," to let the bears know we were coming. I, goofing around as usual, was calling, "Here, bear, here, bear."

The trail wound through lush, deep-green evergreen forests, and the ground was covered with bright green moss. Soon we encountered a beautifully built boardwalk with a very chewed-on gate across it. The boardwalk was wide enough for my wheelchair and one other person to walk side by side. Where the ground level drops, the boardwalk rises a good ten or fifteen feet in the air. Soon we encountered another gate, this one about eight feet tall and made of steel, quite bear-proof. Just past this gate was the boardwalk that went out to the riffles platform, which is only about 150 feet down-river from the falls.

I had been told that since the smaller silver salmon would not be jumping the falls, we would probably be seeing no bears at the falls. I was thrilled, therefore, to see from the riffles platform two boars fishing at the falls. We immediately left the riffles platform for the falls platform, a journey that took all of about two minutes. When we got there, we found not only the two boars fishing the Brooks Falls, but also a sow with three cubs feeding on salmon right under the platform, about fifteen feet below us. It was great!

At the falls platform is a small lower-level platform that can be reached by going down about four steps. All the platforms have heavy forty-three-inch-high railings around them, too high for me to shoot over unaided. But I found if I positioned myself at the top of the steps that lead down to the lower platform, there was no railing to block my view. The railing around the lower platform was below my line of sight, unless I was trying to shoot straight down. I had a perfect unobstructed view of the entire Brooks Falls with two good-sized boars fishing for salmon—and, yes, the silver salmon were jumping the falls.

We all had a great time photographing the bears, and after the bears left, we also decided to call it a night—except that we were stopped on the trail for the next a half hour by two sleeping bears. By the time we made it back to the lodge, it was past dinnertime. At Bev's request, the kitchen saved me some dinner, which was very good, I supposed, but my mind was still back at the falls. It was better than I dreamed it would be. After showing Bev my digital pictures, I burned them to a CD. Before I cleared my memory card though, I just had to look at it a few more times. What a great day it had been! After repeatedly thanking the Lord for everything, I finally cleared the card and tried to get some sleep.

Bev had signed up to take a full-day bus tour to the Valley of Ten Thousand Smokes, so I was on my own the next day. After breakfast, we walked and rolled together to the Point where a large group of people were gathered, once again delayed by sow number 410 and her three cubs taking a nap right in the middle of the trail. Nobody scheduled to go on the tour was worried about missing the bus because the driver was also stuck on the Point. Sow 410 finally woke up and ambled off with her cubs. Everyone going on the tour climbed aboard the bus. The rest of us proceeded across the bridge.

I had on the utility frame mounted with both cameras: my old Nikon F3 hooked up to my 1,000 mm and, next to that, the new Nikon D70 digital camera hooked up to my 300 mm zoom lens. I figured that between these two cameras and lenses of different power, I should be able to capture almost any situation. I also had my Nikon 8008s autofocus hanging around my neck with a 28–80 mm zoom lens attached and ready to swing into action to capture anything that might be happening off to the side in a hurry.

It was a quiet, cool morning with only a few boars and sows with cubs out fishing. More bears would probably be out later as the temperature warmed. The morning passed quickly with enough action going on to keep everybody busy at their cameras. As lunchtime grew near, the crowd of bear watchers thinned out dramatically, and soon there were only a few of us left talking and shooting the bears, who were also eating lunch. Early in the afternoon, I joined two other photographers on a hike to the falls. It was a slow day there also; only one boar, whose nickname is Snaggletooth, was fishing. I took more than a few photos of him and was quite content to just sit there, watching him and listening to the sound of the falls.

Any wildlife photographer will tell you that patience is the key to good photography. I don't care how good you are or how good your equipment is, if the critters don't cooperate, you don't get the shots. But if you sit and wait long enough in the right situation you will probably get the shots you want eventually.

By late afternoon, only one other photographer remained at the falls area. When he decided to leave, I went with him so that I would not be trapped on the boardwalk by the two eight-foot steel mesh gates and the wooden gate. At the lower platforms were a number of sows with cubs, and I decided to stay, not wanting to waste a minute of daylight. Bev showed up to collect me around seven o'clock in the evening. I joined her for dinner, after which I went back to the lower platforms to get some sunset shots.

In the evening, after burning the day's shooting to a CD, I returned to the lodge to chat with some of the other guests. A woman approached me and asked, "Were you in the Chilkat Valley last November?"

I replied, "Yes." Then I remembered: she was on the same tour bus, and one day I saw her out on the ice photographing a four-year-old eagle devouring a salmon. We talked for a while, then said good night. Funny, the people you run into in the middle of nowhere. It made me feel very good and very much at home.

The next morning outside our cabin, as Bev was hooking up the utility frame to my chair, a ranger shouted, "Look out! There's a bear about twenty feet behind you." He was a little three- or four-year-old, only about seven or eight hundred pounds, and he was cute just standing on the trail watching us. Bev was a little shaken, but I was thrilled.

The good mood didn't last long because the day was overcast and drizzling, and it would be my last full day here. I rolled to the Point and waited with few other people being held up by sow 410 and her sleeping cubs. It started raining harder, so I went back to the cabin to get my rain gear, which Bev couldn't find. Jen must have accidentally packed it with her stuff. We waited in the lodge for the rain to stop, and when it did, Bev decided to come with me to see for herself what I had been raving about for a day and a half.

This time we made it all the way to the lower platforms without delay and stayed there several hours before continuing on to the riffles and falls platform. We walked and rolled the rest of the way to the riffles platform without seeing a single bear. When we got there, a sow and two cubs were just leaving. Bev was getting into the spirit of things now, taking photographs of the bears. At the falls platform, a single boar was fishing. After a while another large boar showed up in the falls almost right next to the platform. Because I could not shoot straight down, I couldn't get any shots of him, but Bev could—and did.

When the rain started up again, we headed back to the riffles, which has a small covered area on the boardwalk where people can sit and wait their turns to go out onto the platforms. While waiting, I tried to get a magpie to pose for me. No luck. He must have been camera shy.

The rain let up a bit, and we started back, making it as far as the lower platform, where about eight or ten other people were being held back by none other than 410 and her cubs sleeping by the Point. It was getting to be the dinner hour. People were getting jittery. Imes was the ranger on watch at the lower platform and, of course, he'd been in radio contact with other rangers, keeping tabs on the location of bears. At around 6:30, Imes was given the all-clear to use a small alternate trail that cut diagonally through a part of the somewhat dry marsh around the Point. Bev and the other ambulatory bear watchers were able to get back to the lodge.

Since this trail was definitely not wheelchair accessible, I remained behind. Imes stayed with me, and we had the next two hours to talk about bears, the Katmai, my dreams of getting up close to study the bears, and just about everything else. Soon enough, we were both soaked and chilled to the bone. But at least my cameras were protected by plastic garbage bags. Imes radioed to the kitchen to save me a dinner plate, and I thanked him. Finally, sow 410 and her cubs woke up and wandered out onto the trail, but she didn't leave, and we were still trapped in the middle of the floating bridge where you are normally not allowed to stop. It was just Imes and I and bears all around us, fishing. It was wonderful! I looked down into the crystal-clear water and was amazed to see thousands upon thousands of brightly colored ten- or twelve-pound salmon—no wonder the bears are so fat and healthy.

Finally around eight o'clock, sow 410 decided to go fishing and walked with one of her cubs almost to the end of the bridge and into the water about twenty feet off shore. Imes called Joel Ellis on the radio and was given the okay to make a break for it. We exited the bridge and turned onto the trail. The other two cubs, about 150 to 200 pounds each, were sitting at the water's edge half a dozen feet away. Imes knew I wanted to stop and watch, but he told me, "Just keep moving, as fast as possible." We made it back to the lodge without further delay, but I was so bone-chilled it took me a good fifteen minutes to stop shivering. They brought me a dinner plate, and every time I picked up a knife to cut the baby red potatoes, I dropped it because my hands were so cold.

In all the trips I have taken, I have never had weather bad enough to keep me from shooting photos. The only weather that bothers me is rain, but today, even that turned out to be a blessing. If not for the rain, the rangers wouldn't have been so worried about getting me back inside. We would have stayed up on the safe platform far from the bears instead of in the middle of the bridge—sometimes with bears as close as ten feet away. Thanks to Imes, who stuck with me on that cold wet bridge, I got to observe these bears much closer than I otherwise would have been allowed, thanks to 410.

All in all, this had been the best rainy day of my life.

The next day was our last here. After breakfast in the dining hall, I decided to take only my digital camera with my 28–80 mm zoom lens to do a little documentary photography of the floating bridge, the platforms, and ramps. I made my way down to an open area of beachfront and photographed the most beautiful sunrise I ever saw over the mountains on the other side of the lake. Next, I made my way down to the Point, where I joined the usual crowd of photographers who were being held up by 410 and her sleeping cubs. This morning especially brought to mind just how much I feel like I belong here, more than any other place I have ever been. Here, life revolves around the whims of nature. Nobody complains about being held up by sleeping bears or the rain like we had yesterday; they just enjoy it. And aside from comments about the "bear-icades" on the trail, or the wait being "un-bear-able," the only real sound you hear is the clicking of many cameras every time 410 or one of her cubs looks up before returning to sleep.

This is an example of what I mean about everything here revolving around nature. At the Point, I was talking with another photographer, when he said suddenly, "What's that behind you?" I turned to look, and hopping around on the trail about three feet away was a shrew, about the size of a large grape. Here we were, a dozen photographers who had come from all over the world to photograph one of the largest land carnivores in the world, and suddenly everyone was either sitting or kneeling or lying on their bellies trying to photograph a tiny shrew, the littlest "bear" on the Katmai. Because I was stuck way up here in my wheelchair, I set my lens to macro, adjusted the rest of the settings and handed the camera to a photographer who was on his belly; he got me a couple of good close shots. The whole episode was wonderful. Everybody loved trying to photograph this tiny, normally shy creature. Nobody said, "No big deal, it's just a mouse." If there's anywhere in the world I would gladly spend the rest of my life, it's here at the Brooks Camp, Katmai National Park.

Since this was the last day the camp would be open this year (it closes on the seventeenth for the winter), Joel Ellis and Imes decided to wake sow 410 and her cubs so we could get to the platforms. Carefully they approached, and when they were about fifteen feet away, they blew their air horns. All the bear did was lift her massive head, look at them, yawn, and lie back down, provoking some good laughter from the delighted crowd. After all, she was practicing for winter hibernation. The rangers don't like to roust bears: not only is it somewhat dangerous, but if done too often, the bears grow tolerant of people, and that's when trouble starts. Imes and Joel gave up on the air horn, but Joel picked up a couple of sticks and banged them together. Evidently, sow 410 didn't appreciate Joel's rhythm. She woke her cubs, and they wandered off.

By this time, I decided not to cross the bridge, figuring if 410 or some other sow with cubs decided to sleep on the trail again, I would be trapped on the wrong side of the bridge. Sure enough, fifteen minutes later, 410 and her cubs were back to their favorite sleeping spot.

I stayed at the Point talking with Imes and Joel, and then I went to find Bev. Packed and ready to leave, we said our good-byes and went to wait for the floatplane, which arrived right on time. Joel and another ranger transferred me to a kitchen chair. Joel and Dave Wagner, the pilot, dismantled my chair and stowed it in the plane. Then they carried me over and hoisted me into the plane. After Bev climbed in, Dave ran over the safety procedures again, and with a final good-bye to Joel and a thank-you to everyone there, we took off for King Salmon

When we arrived at King Salmon, I was picked up and carried to a chair that was sitting on the pier; our gear was unloaded and my chair reassembled. I was then transferred to my chair and assisted up the long boat ramp. The Quinnat Hotel was unable to pick us up so Van Hartley, owner and operator of Branch River Air Service, again transported us, but this time, he managed to get me into the passenger seat of the big four-by-four. We made it to the airport in plenty of time for our 5:15 flight.

Once back in Anchorage, I called the hotel where we had reservations, and they assured me they would send an access ible courtesy car. We waited nearly an hour for the car, and when it arrived, we saw it wasn't accessible. We waited another hour for a wheelchair-accessible taxi.

Though it was a short night, I rested, pleased with the way things had gone on the trip. Except for the first two days, the weather was flawless, and as I said, even the rain on the fifteenth turned out to be a blessing.

The taxi was a little late getting us to the airport, but we made our flight. Now we were back to the standard transfer by the door of the plane in the Jetway. A few of the flight attendants remembered me and asked about the trip. All I could say is that it was the best trip of my lifetime, even though we had bad weather on the second day, causing the Kenia Fjords tour to be cancelled. Perhaps, the Lord holds some things back from us, so that when He finally presents them to us we will better appreciate them. Maybe next time…if there is a next time—and I pray that there is, provided that is what the Lord wants me to do. The Lord's will, not mine.

For a few days, I wondered if I had failed the Lord by not talking to Bev and Jen about Him. The most I had done was to say to them the evening after the moose, "I think we need to thank the Lord for all He has shown us today." But that is all I said. I should have asked them to join me in prayer, but I didn't, and that is why I thought I failed the Lord. I was reminded by two very close friends that if the Lord had wanted me to say something, He would have put the words into my mouth. I still have a great deal to learn, and I hope I never stop learning.

You may ask, as I have asked myself, now that I am a believer, why doesn't God heal me physically? I think I have the answer. I don't know if it's the right answer because nobody knows the mind of God. I have often thought, what would I do if I were miraculously healed of all my physical problems? Would I revert to my old ways? God forbid! Besides, I like living with my newly discovered faith and trust and feelings of love and humanity. Just think what a great impact it would make on everyone who might be on the brink of accepting Jesus Christ into their lives if they could learn about someone like me who was all of a sudden miraculously healed, as good as new. It would definitely make a great impact. But would it have a lasting impact?

Maybe God has in his plans something different for me, something that is not as spectacular, but might have a deeper, longer-lasting impression. I'm not going to try to second-guess God, but my human logic hopes this. Maybe this book and my photography are the key. If I were healed right now, my trips to Alaska and wherever else the Lord prompts me to go in the future would be no big deal. Many photographers go to Alaska every year. I would be just one more shutterbug. But as I see it, I'm possibly the first to tackle the Katmai and the giant Coastal Alaska Brown Bears while confined to an electric wheelchair. Also if I were healed, it could definitely cause those sinful emotions: jealousy, envy, and even despair to spring up in some other disabled people. Why was he healed and not me? I pray that reading about this trip and my other travels will be a positive experience for everybody.

I had worked long and hard planning this trip. And I'd held on to this Alaska dream for thirty-six years. I hope that anyone reading this realizes that if I can do it from a wheelchair, anyone in a wheelchair can do it if they truly want to. I'm sure more than a few people are held back from completing their dreams because of self-doubt or fears, especially the fear of failure, just as I was afraid to pick up my camera for a while because I was afraid that I might not be able to do it anymore. But once I tried and took my time, everything was okay. I know that whenever I saw other photographic works of Alaska, I said to myself, I would like to see what I could do if only I could get there, but I'm stuck here in this wheelchair. Seeing these other photographic works strengthened my resolve and imprinted on my mind the beauty that is just waiting there to be captured—by your mind's eye or by a camera.

All you can do is hold on to your dreams and work for them any way you can. If you can't take a photograph, perhaps you can paint or draw. Maybe you can write about it or maybe simply describe it to someone who can't see or tell stories about it to children to give them dreams.

From what I had seen in Southeast Alaska on my first trip, plus all that the Lord shared with me on this trip. God knows how much I love the outdoors, but if I had made it there before my accident and before I knew the Lord, I never would have been able to return to the Lower 48. I might still be running around up there seeing all that beauty but never really feeling the true beauty of God's creation.

BACK TO CHILKAT

I returned to Chilkat Valley in November 2005, accompanied by Amy Berta. I just had to go back there one more time to photograph the eagles again. This time, I would be using my new high-speed, light-weight, more versatile digital camera. I prayed over and over again that the weather for this trip be as perfect as the first trip.

We never saw the sun. Monday was very overcast but otherwise clear. Tuesday snowed all day from early morning until evening. This gave everything a fresh clean whiteness, but it made photography from a wheelchair somewhat difficult because I was having trouble moving around by midmorning. Wednesday was again very overcast but clear of rain or snow until about one thirty in the afternoon. At about that time on Wednesday, it started to rain, a fairly steady but sometimes heavy rain, and it didn't stop raining until almost two days after we returned home. Usually rain is the one weather condition that completely destroys my mood to do anything outside, especially photography. This time something very different happened. Instead of getting all flustered and in a foul mood, I simply said okay, I'll just get into the bus and shoot through the open side door. Actually this turned out to be sometimes advantageous because shooting from inside the bus put me at a much higher level of view. I no longer had to worry about all the brush that grows along the riverside, sometimes taller than I am, many times interfering with the shots. I later found out that this is the normal weather for Southeast Alaska in November, where it rains about six out of ten days. It made me appreciate even more the miracle of the absolutely perfect weather I had on my first trip here.

What the Lord didn't do for us in the weather department He more than made up for it in the eagle department. I was totally amazed by the eagles that I saw on the first trip. Now there were at least three to four times as many. Eagles everywhere—on the snow covered trees or on the riverbanks, but mostly on every downed tree or branch all across the valley floor. Hundreds upon hundreds of eagles, completely amazing. On Wednesday before the rain started, I tried to do something that I have always wanted to do but was never able to do because of the limitations of my camera equipment combined with my limitations of movement. I started shooting eagles in flight, not just eagles soaring far away high in the sky, but eagles up close enough to see the pupils of their eyes. I photographed them landing, taking off, flying low over the water, and just about every way I could think of. With my new high-speed autofocus camera, this was almost easy. I still think that I must have fallen asleep and the Lord was taking the pictures for me because many of the shots I got are amazing. I took a total of 1,480 photographs that week, in spite of the somewhat dismal weather, and after eliminating all shots that were somewhat out of focus, blurred, or because I just did not like the pose of the eagle or the lighting on its face, I still have about 850 good, workable new eagle photographs.

NEW CHAPTER IN MY LIFE

In early 2004, I stopped in at the new Algonquin public library just to check it out and found out that they had the walker hanging system there for displaying art work. I thought that this might be a great opportunity to display some of my work, and when I inquired at the desk, I was assigned a two-month span of November and December. This would be a perfect time to display some of the new shots from my upcoming dream trip in September. Amy and I set up my exhibit called *Visions of Alaska* on the first of November.

My exhibit and my Alaskan trip attracted local newspaper reporter Allison Smith to write a short piece about my wildlife photography. Allison was among several journalists to seek me out over the years, and she took her continued interest to an unprecedented level. Allison and her friend Stephanie Book both love documentaries and were watching one while sitting on Allison's red couch. Intrigued with my story and my photography, they formed Red Couch Productions and decided that they would like to try to do a documentary on me, with Allison writing the documentary and Stephanie doing the camera work. Allison approached me with this idea, and I thought it would be interesting. She is now working to make a cinéma vérité (intimate, real life, no narration) about me, both on my daily life and my potential travels in the future. Allison and Red Couch Productions felt that my story should be told. To this end, spurred on by the thought of this documentary, I toyed with the idea of trying to live out one of my other photography dreams, traveling up to Churchill, Canada, to the very edge of the Arctic Circle to photograph polar bears in the wild. I had checked into this many years ago, just daydreaming, but almost completely abandoned the thought as just too expensive and, in my thoughts at the time, impossible to do in my situation.

While discussing this documentary and talking about my photographic dreams, I explained to Allison that it took me about thirty-six years to save up enough money for this dream trip to Alaska and that there was no way that I could afford another trip back there or anywhere else in the foreseeable future, let alone tackling something as expensive as Churchill. Allison explained that we should be able to do this at no cost to me. I figured that Allison would be getting backers for the documentary and that would pay for everything. This was a dream come true—to be able to travel and photograph both the great Alaskan coastal brown bears again and the greatest of all land carnivores, the polar bear, and not cost me anything? Just don't wake me up.

We started figuring out the best dates as to when these two trips should be taken. Allison and Stephanie did some local shooting of me in order to make a five-minute trailer video to show potential investors. They also did some interviews of friends. It was during one of these interviews that the title for the documentary was born. During one such interview, Fred Becker, a friend from our small church paraphrased from the book of Proverbs: "A lazy man says, 'There is a lion in the street. I might get killed.' But David is the opposite of that." Jokingly he said,

"David would go out looking for the lion." Hence came the title of the documentary *Lion in the Street*.

After a concert one evening, Amy, Allison, and Stephanie, and I were out for a light dinner. Allison told me the title for the documentary. It didn't even occur to me that it was from the proverb; instead I immediately replied, "Yes, I was lyin' on the street after my accident." Allison said that she hadn't even thought of that aspect.

Next Allison and Stephanie enlisted a friend of theirs to help set up the website www.lioninthestreet.com so people could learn more about the documentary and follow its progress and hopefully make donations to the project.

I gave Allison the names of all the contacts that I had made from my 2004 trip, and she was working on her end of the project, trying to get in-kind donations of reduced fares, etc. I was busy doing what I always do for even the smallest trip—researching everything that I can in order to become completely familiar with the area in which I am going. I was still somewhat skeptical about the possibility of Churchill, Canada. Now with the great success of my Alaska adventures, I began to think, "Maybe it's not so impossible after all. If this is what the Lord wants me to do, then He will make it all possible."

Allison was hard at work and talked the Alaska Airlines people into reducing our fares for the Alaska trip. She also talked to Van Hartley at Branch River Air Service, and he agreed to greatly reduce the fee of the floatplane. Allison talked to the people at the Best Western Hotel in Anchorage, and they donated the two rooms we would need for the one night there. After conversations with Allison, Sony Petersen at Katmailand agreed to donate the use of two cabins for two nights at the Brooks Camp. The manager at the Quinatt Hotel on King Salmon agreed to give us the rooms at half price, so basically all we would have to pay for on this Alaska trip was the reduced fare transportation, our stay at the Quinatt Hotel, and food. The nights Katmailand donated to us were August 27 and 28, 2006. This was a little earlier in the season than I had gone in 2004, so I figured that the cubs would be a full two weeks younger and much smaller and cuter, a better photographic opportunity .

Everything was going along smoothly when Allison dropped the bomb on me just four months before the scheduled Alaska trip. Although there were many in-kind donations and Merv and Lynda Gunter at Frontiers North in Churchill put together a special package for us for the trip there and reduced the price by half for the documentary, ethically, they could not just hand me my dream trip to Churchill, Canada. Part of the documentary was to show how I must work to make these dream trips come true. The proposed budget for these two trips for my caregiver, Amy, and I came to a whopping $10,000. How was I supposed to raise that kind of money in just four months? I thought she was nuts. I just couldn't do it.

Allison helped me to write a letter that I could mail out to friends and business contacts asking for donations. I have never before in my life asked anybody for a donation of any kind for anything, let alone for a trip to Alaska and Churchill. I rewrote the letter a few times before sending it out to anyone. Finally, I was satisfied with how it read and mailed out about sixty-five letters. I also e-mailed out about another forty letters, which friends forwarded to other friends and acquaintances. I prayed and sat back and waited, not really thinking that anybody would actually donate anything. I was floored when I got my first letter containing a very nice donation of $250 and a letter of encouragement back just a week after I had mailed out the letters. This was from a friend that I had not seen or heard from in a number of years. I started receiving return letters and donations about every other day. Almost all the donations came with very nice letters of encouragement that were almost more important to me than the donations themselves.

Things were going well, but I still wasn't sure that I could raise that much money in that short a period of time. After about two months, the donations were coming in at a good, steady pace. I continued to praise the Lord for every donation that I received, and overall, it was very humbling and at the same time uplifting to know that everyone had such faith in my ability to pull this trip off. It was then that I received three donations in a row for $500 each, two from friends and one from a cousin. This really blew my mind. It had been twenty-two years since I worked a full-time job, and right now $500 seemed like an awful lot of money to donate to me so that I could live out my dream. I was still not even to the halfway mark and began to wonder if this is what the Lord really wanted me to do. I found myself praying more than I ever had in my life. About this time, I received an e-mail from friends out east telling me that they would like to make a $1,500 donation. To say the least, I was elated. This would put me very near the halfway mark. Then right around the beginning of June, I received a letter telling me that I had been approved for a $1,500 grant from the Illinois Arts Council. Next, I received a letter and donation that really brought tears to my eyes. The letter was from a friend's brother, whom I had met only once at my friends fiftieth wedding anniversary party. With the letter was a check that at first glance, through the tears blurring my vision, I thought was for another $500. Fantastic—hey wait a minute. There are too many zeros. The check was for an unbelievable $5,000. I still can't read the letter without tears of gratitude and joy coming to my eyes.

Dear David,

I feel as if I know you very well. Brother Wes keeps me informed of all your activities, and Wes tells me inspiring things about your life. Not the least that he tells me that you have made a commitment to becoming a Christian. You have more courage and intestinal fortitude than is normally possible for only a very few humans. You are in a very special class and we want to give you our complete trust that you have found your reason for living and we want to help you in your endeavors.

All our love,
Jim

Mike was our son who died last January at age 51. He left some money for us and we can't see a better use for it than to aid you.

I no longer had any doubt that this is what the Lord wanted me to do.

Now with only a month to go before the first trip, I had the money that I needed for both trips. Now the only thing holding up the show was the funding for the Red Couch Productions group. Ethically, Allison couldn't hand me my dream trip to Churchill and on the same ethical note couldn't accept any money from me for the documentary. With great thanks, Allison received a five-thousand-dollar grant from the Christopher Reeve Foundation.

This grant gave them at least enough money to complete the first trip. With just three weeks to go, I called the Quinatt Hotel just to confirm that everything was set for our arrival in King Salmon. What a shock it was to find out that there had been a fire and the Quinnat Hotel had burned to the ground. Luckily, I panicked for only a couple of minutes before calling Katmailand. I spoke to Melissa, the person I had been in communication with for so long before my 2004 trip. After chatting about what had happened at the Quinnat, I asked if she knew the names of any other hotels in King Salmon. There were only a couple of other hotels, and I immediately called them both to check on room availability, accessibility, and cost. One was not accessible, the other, the King Ko Inn had cabins, one of which was accessible and available for the date we needed. The cost would be about twice what we would have paid at the Quinnat, with our 50 percent discount. I spoke to the manager-owner, Jennifer Quimby and tentatively booked the cabin which is set up to sleep four. With all of us sharing one cabin and splitting the cost, it would be about equal to the cost of the Quinnat. After Allison talked to Jennifer at the King Ko Inn, Jennifer agreed to donate the cabin to us for the documentary. This was another savings of $150 each.

With great excitement Allison, Stephanie, Amy, and I left for Anchorage on August 25. A few of the flight attendants knew me from previous flights, so the transfers from my wheelchair to the aisle chair and then to my assigned seat went without a hitch.

The Lord was again at work in our favor. I only hoped that He would continue to favor us on this trip. We arrived in Anchorage in the late evening, only to wait a couple of hours for the wheelchair-accessible taxi to arrive. It seems that someone had hired the only accessible taxi to go bar hopping for a couple hours. We finally made it to the hotel and caught a few hours of restless sleep. I was hoping nothing would hold up the taxi this morning so that we could make our flight to King Salmon. I was a little worried about the weather in the King Salmon and Brooks Camp area. During phone conversations with Van Hartley at Branch River Air, I'd learned that they had been and were having about the worse weather they ever had. So far, they had had seven weeks of almost continuous rain, not all day, but everyday rain and fog. The small air transport companies like Branch River Air were really hurting right now because they had been forced to cancel, due to the rain and fog, many of their short fly in and pick up flights for those fishermen who only want to fly in somewhere for a day of fishing.

We made it to the airport in plenty of time only to find out that our flight was delayed about an hour due to fog. Since Allison had been in communication with the powers that be at Alaska Air about the documentary, when we finally boarded the plane, we were given a very royal kind of treatment. First we were bumped from economy up to first-class seating. Then during the flight, the captain made an announcement over the intercom about the documentary and really made us feel like celebrities. We arrived in King Salmon in good weather and walked—in my case, rolled—to the King Ko Inn, which was only about one hundred yards away from the small airport terminal. We got checked in to a very nice comfortable cabin, and Amy and I decided to take a walk to see how long it would take us to go the mile or so to Branch River Air so we would know how much time to give ourselves the next morning since we were planning on walking and rolling there for our flight to Brooks camp. Mary Ann, a woman who works at the Alaska Air terminal happened to be walking the opposite direction at that time, and we struck up a conversation. She asked us where we were off to, so we told her that we were just checking out how long it would take us to get to Branch River air because we would have to walk and roll there tomorrow morning to catch our plane.

She said, "Why, that's ridiculous. I think that the retirement center has a wheelchair-accessible vehicle. Let me make a few calls, and I'll call you this evening."

Well, Mary Ann, was true to her word and called that evening. She had talked to her boss at Alaska Air and had arranged for them to use their brand new DPL to transport me to Branch River Air. The DPL was there waiting for me at 6:30 a.m. the next morning. They loaded Amy and I up and drove very carefully over the very rutted dirt road the mile or so to Branch River Air. It looked like it was going to be a perfect day. Van Hartley said that yesterday, the day we arrived, and today were the first days in weeks that they had no rain. One benefit to all the rain they had had was that the water levels were very high and the very steep ramp down to the floating pier seemed not so steep this time. Since we were using the same small Cessna that we used in 2004. It was decided that Stephanie and I would take the first flight to Brooks camp. We would then wait while the plane went back for Amy and Allison. After all our gear was stowed away in our respective cabins, we all attended bear school, after which I could wait no longer to go out to see and photograph the bears. With all the rain over the past six weeks, the water level of the river was way up. There was some damage from erosion to the trail that runs along the river from the point to the floating bridge. Part of the trail was closed off, but I was allowed to use it if I stayed as far from the water edge as possible. The other drawback to the very high water was one I had not counted on. As I said before, the cubs would be a full two weeks younger and much smaller than my first trip. Unfortunately, there were no cubs to be seen, not one the entire trip. This made my first trip here all that much more of a blessing, with the dozen or so cubs that I been blessed with the opportunity to observe and photograph. The two-week difference did have a different benefit. The silver salmon run had not kicked into full gear, and there were still some huge, bright-red sockeye salmon gathered at the Brooks Falls. I was fortunate enough to see a large bear fishing at the falls, dive in, and come up with a brilliant red twenty- to thirty-pound sockeye in its mouth. When I saw this, I was on the riffles platform so the photo I got has the roaring Brooks Falls behind as a background. Allison and Stephanie said they got about eleven hours of good footage for the documentary. Now comes the very tedious job of documenting every bit of film, only then can they decide what parts to actually use in the documentary. At the end of our stay at Brooks camp, Branch River Air was there at the appointed time. This time, Amy and I took the first flight, then the pilot would return for Allison and Stephanie. We were all treated to a special treat. Instead of flying at the normal high altitude, the pilot took us on a low-flying scenic trip back to King Salmon, flying just high enough to safely clear the trees.

After seven weeks of rain, we had been blessed with three consecutive days of flawless weather. When Amy and I arrived back at Branch River air we had another nice surprise. There was a nice new bus complete with a wheelchair lift waiting for us. Mary Ann had made more phone calls and talked to the woman who drove the bus for the retirement center. She needed a break from painting her kitchen, so she agreed to pick us up and drive us to the airport terminal. Branch River Air would bring Allison and Stephanie with all their gear when they arrived from Brooks Camp.

The second trip to Churchill had to be postponed until next year because the grants that Red Couch productions had applied for failed to come in. Because of that, I was forced to withdraw my request for the grant from the Illinois Arts Council. I have reapplied for the grant this year and can only pray that Red Couch Productions receives the funds this year.

The trip to Churchill is scheduled for October 15–20, 2007.

It's kind of funny in a way, how things work when the Lord is doing all the work. During the fundraising time for me, at times I was more than just a little disappointed. Those whom I got a lot of encouragement from and who were professionals making good money were the ones who gave less. But the point I'm trying to make is there was no need for me to feel hurt because they chose not to donate or for me to count on their donations at all because the Lord saw to it that I had more than enough for both trips.

It was in the beginning of September when I received an e-mail invoice for the remainder of the funds due for the Churchill trip. Now the pressure was on me because I had not heard from Allison as to whether or not they had finally received any of the funding they would need to complete the trip to Churchill, Canada. After a couple frustrating days of failed tries at contacting Allison, I finally reached her. She had been very busy planning their final arrangements for the trip, and she explained that Red Couch Productions had received the necessary funding for this final trip.

Thank God. We still had about five weeks to go, but I knew it would go by in the blink of an eye.

It was a bright crisp mid-October morning when Amy and I headed to O'Hare airport to catch our flight to Winnipeg, Manitoba, Canada. This was a little bit of a different experience for me because I had never flown out of the country before. This was the first time I had ever had to use a passport. We arrived in Winnipeg fairly early in the day, so Amy and I headed out on a little excursion to check out the Winnipeg zoo. I had hoped to get a few shots of an adult Canadian lynx. It was a nice outing, but photographically, it was a waste of time. The lynx exhibit was very primitive compared to some of our zoos. The somewhat small exhibit was nothing like I had hoped for by way of a natural-looking habitat, kind of barren with a log on the ground where the lynx was sleeping, surrounded by double mesh chain-link fencing—no way possible to shoot photos through that kind of fence. At closing time, we left and caught the wheelchair-accessible taxi back to the hotel and had dinner in the hotel restaurant.

The next morning between 6:00 and 6:30 a.m., the wheelchair transport vehicle was at the hotel to pick us up and drive us back to a completely different part of the airfield.

This was a much smaller airplane, a fifty-or-so passenger prop plane. Instead of boarding through a Jetway, as we did for a bigger plane, we just walked out on the tarmac, and everybody except me climbed up the stairway to the plane. They had no aisle chair available so two of the flight crew picked me up and carried me up the stairs and into my seat. Upon arrival in Churchill, the same two flight crew people carried me down the flight of stairs to my waiting wheelchair.

Frontiers North, the polar bear tour people had made an arrangement with a retirement home to use their accessible transport bus for the time I was to be there; unfortunately there was a mix-up as to when my arrival time was. So there was no way to get me to the hotel from the small airfield. I talked to Merve, the owner of Frontiers North, and said that it didn't really matter to me about the comfort of the bus, so we improvised some long ramps, and Amy and I rode in the baggage truck from the airfield to the hotel.

After we were all checked into the hotel and all the baggage was unloaded, the crew from Frontiers North asked if we would like to be shown around. We said yes, so Amy and I went back up the long ramps into the baggage truck, and off we went. The crew took us out to Fort Churchill and gave us a short tour. Nice scenery, but unfortunately no polar bears. After our little tour, we headed back to the hotel to meet up with Allison and Stephanie for dinner.

Allison and Stephanie had flown up a few days earlier to see and film some of the modification work being done on the Tundra Buggy. The modifications were quite extensive. All the seats, except the first three rows, in the large bus-like vehicle built on an old fire engine chassis were removed to make ample room for my wheelchair to freely move around. The next main modification was the windows. All the windows in the buggy open from the top down, and the bottom edge of the open window was fifty-six inches up off the floor of the buggy. There was no way that I could reach up that high to photograph out an open window.

After promising that I would not try to pet any of the cute polar bears, two windows, one on each side of the buggy, were turned over so that they opened from the bottom up. Now the bottom of the window was only about thirty-eight inches up from the floor of the buggy and even I could reach that comfortably. There was no need to really worry because the floor of the tundra buggy is about eleven feet up from the ground, so now the bottom of the open window was still about fourteen feet up from the ground. It would take a very large polar bear to reach up that high. We only saw one bear that big and he was sleeping and not interested in us whatsoever.

The next morning at 7:00 a.m. sharp, the nice new wheelchair-accessible bus was there at the hotel to pick us up for our first full day out on the tundra. The ride out to the launch was about twenty-five miles from Churchill. It was a beautiful drive, and the sun rose when we were about halfway there. Perfect morning.

I had been in almost constant communication with the crew doing the modifications to the tundra buggy, and we had discussed the best way to get me up on the launch platform, which is about ten feet high. Building a ramp system was, in my opinion, just not practical. It would have been to dangerous if it snowed. After much discussion, I suggested that they just bring a sturdy kitchen-type chair out to the launch.

After meeting everyone who had done the modifications, we met our guide driver for the three days, Glen Hopfner.

I positioned my wheelchair next to the kitchen chair and two of the crew lifted me out of my chair, onto the kitchen chair. That transfer done, four guys picked up my 265-pound wheelchair and carried it up to the launch platform. Then they came back down for me.

They leaned the chair far back then picked up the chair with me and carried me up to the platform, then transferred me back into my wheelchair. I then rolled right into the tundra buggy under my own power. It was a very smooth transfer from wheelchair to kitchen chair, back to wheelchair, and into the tundra buggy.

It was finally time to start, and we headed out into the Wapusk National Park. Boy, was I ever in for a surprise. I guess that in my daydreaming about the Wapusk, I had thought it would be somewhat like our national parks. I knew that the tundra buggies drove around the area, so I guess I imagined that there would be man-made gravel roads. I had convinced the Frontiers North people not to try to lock my wheelchair down in any way so that I would have complete freedom of movement to look around and photograph out of either side of the buggy at a moments notice. On the Wapusk, there are no man-made gravel roads or even trails. The tundra buggies follow trails that are just narrow areas where the natural loam (top soil) has been worn away by the winds and the only smooth spots are when the tundra buggy is balanced upon a boulder for a few seconds before it comes crashing down again. Even moving only a couple miles an hour, it was all I could do to hold onto the back of the last seat toward the front of the bus. Talk about bumpy, even the road in front of my house isn't that bad, and it has been slated for resurfacing for the last four years. My wheelchair was airborne a few inches more than a couple times; lucky for me, I wear my seatbelt nice and tight.

Spending a good portion of my life on the lookout for wildlife, I thought that I would be able to be the first to spot much of the wildlife on this trip. Wrong again, I don't think that I was the first to spot anything except maybe a snow bunting a couple of times. Glen stopped to point out our first polar bear, and I felt blind, how could I not be able to see a huge polar bear almost right in front of my eyes. He was sleeping by the edge of a tidal pool, and I thought it was a just another large boulder. Glen commented on how flawless this weather was for this time of year. There is normally a twenty- to thirty-mile per hour wind howling across the open subarctic tundra. We had three days of perfectly still air, with not so much as a hint of a breeze.

The tidal pools were all like absolute mirrors. I took many photos of the scenic beauty with perfect reflections of trees and rocks in the water. Overall I took about 250 photos that first day on the tundra. We saw many polar bears (though always only one at a time) and ptarmigan (the largest of the grouse family) in its full white winter plumage. The only other wildlife that I photographed on that first day was snow buntings.

By the end of the day, my arm felt like it weighed a ton, and I was exhausted, but I still felt wonderful.

The second day started out exactly like the first day. We had perfectly clear weather with not even a hint of a breeze. Glen, our guide, and I had talked, and he knew that I would love to try to get a few shots of a white gyrfalcon, the largest falcon in North America. These birds are commonly seen on the Wapusk in the winter season. We headed out toward a point to the east on the very edge of Hudson Bay where Glen thought I would have my best chance of seeing one. We didn't see any gyrfalcons, but we did see and get fairly close, about fifty feet, from an immature peregrine falcon. I got some great shots of this bird perched on a boulder overlooking the perfectly blue waters of the Hudson Bay. We looked around that area a little while longer but found no other wildlife to photograph. On the way back toward the areas more likely to have polar bear sightings, we saw more ptarmigan plus we saw a few Arctic hares, and I was able to get some nice photographs of them.

By around noon we were back in the area where there were quite a few polar bears. I had hoped for at least a light dusting of snow for effect, but the Lord knew what would make a more dramatic photo. Photographs of polar bears in the snow are a dime a dozen. I had no idea that this subarctic tundra would be so colorful. Everywhere you looked, there were boulders just covered with lichens of all different colors, reds, oranges even shades of blue. There were large patches of fireweed, which bloom a bright purple in summer, and now even dried up in the winter season, they were still a mild purple. One of my favorite shots from the trip is a polar bear profile standing just off to the side of a large boulder covered in red lichens, and it makes a beautiful contrast. I got another shot of an angled profile, and it looked like the bear was standing in a rainbow of small rocks covered in many different colors. I got shots of polar bears standing between large patches of fireweed, even got one shot that looks like the polar bear was stopping to sniff the fireweed. It was not quite dusk when Glen stopped the tundra buggy to point out a polar bear on a ridge about 250 feet away. I couldn't quite hear what Glen was saying, but supposedly, it was a sow with a cub. I couldn't see the cub even looking through my 400 mm lens. I was taking some photos when the sow started walking forward. Then I saw the cub; he had been sitting directly behind her and now he was all by himself facing right at the tundra buggy with me shooting away. When the sow was about ten or fifteen feet away, the cub all of a sudden kind of woke up, looked around, and you could just imagine him saying, "Hey, wait for me." Then he took off after his mama at a fast waddle. When the cub caught up with the sow, he followed her for a short distance, with me shooting photos the whole time. The sow stopped and turned to face the tundra buggy, and the cub stood right next to her. This whole sequence was quite a beautiful photo op. Then the sow did the most beautiful thing I could imagine. She laid down in a sphinx pose facing the tundra buggy, and the cub climbed up on her back to keep warm. He was also facing the tundra buggy. I took a great many photos during that sequence. It was starting to get dark, so the shots came out a little grainy, but they bring back some great memories. The rest of the ride back to the launch was uneventful, but I felt like I was floating on the air. What a blessing this day had been.

That evening after I had burned all the days' photos to CDs and transferred out of my wheelchair to stretch out on the bed for a little while, Allison and Stephanie came to the door to let Amy and I know that there was a very nice aurora borealis outside. I tried to get back up into my chair, but I just didn't have the strength. My arm felt like lead, so I missed my chance at a good photo op.

A front had come through during the night, and we awoke on the third and last day in Churchill, Canada, to a somewhat heavy fog, and this gave the Wapusk an eerie effect. When the sun rose, some of the fog burned off. It was another totally breezeless day. This day we decided to devote entirely to the polar bears and headed out to the area most frequently visited by the bears. We saw many bears, but again. only one at a time, except for once when there were two bears, both on the shore area, but they were keeping their distance from each other. I was blessed and got a few good shots of a polar bear crossing a tidal pool on some boulders with a nice reflection.

In the early afternoon, we came across this huge polar bear resting on the rocky shore, so Glen parked the tundra buggy about thirty feet away, and we sat and watched him for a while. There were a few other bears in the immediate area, and I was hoping for some kind of confrontation, but they all kept their distance from this huge monster of a bear. During the whole time we sat and watched him, he never got fully to his feet. A few times he sat up halfway, looked around some, yawned and then laid back down for more nap time. We had been in this area watching for some action for about an hour and a half when Glen got a call on the buggy radio. All of a sudden, the whole atmosphere changed. The call was about a couple of younger bears over the next ridge starting to act aggressively toward each other. We got there along with about eleven other tundra buggies and joined a large circle of onlookers. We watched as two, approximately five-year-old, bears started a sparring match, standing up facing each other and fighting with mock ferocity. They would fight for a few minutes standing up, then wrestle on the ground for a few minutes, and then they would all of a sudden just take a break and start nuzzling each other like the best of friends. Then they would separate and start the whole thing over again. When they had finally finished their sparring match and wandered off in opposite directions, it was time for us to start heading back to the launch, leaving us with time to stop on the way, should something come along to photograph. We saw nothing else that day to photograph, so we headed straight back with a great feeling of elation and thanksgiving. What an amazing sequence of photos this was, and what a way to end a totally fantastic photographic adventure. I had taken 167 photos during that sparing session, and looking at them on the camera viewer, they looked great. Overall on that three-day tundra buggy adventure, I shot just over 1,200 photos.

A LOUD AND
CLEAR ANSWER
TO MY PRAYERS

I have had the most amazing month (June 2008). I was nominated and was chosen by the Illinois Rehabilitation Association to receive a statewide personal achievement award for my work in photography and for the assistance I give to Dr. Murray Fisher in teaching teachers and future teachers how to better work with special needs students. The award was a very nice plaque. Because of the photography aspect of the award, I was offered a part-time job shooting photos for the State of Illinois Department of Human Services. I was traveling limited distances within northern Illinois to photograph different functions and people that the state wants to feature in their annual DHS report calendar. For this job, the state paid me $300 per person/photo session plus expenses.

I had my first art show of the season on June 7 and 8. It was really windy all day Saturday, and then on Sunday, we only had about an hour and a half before the storms hit, wiping out the show. I had no storm damage and had done okay sales wise on Saturday. and then got real lucky Sunday. Just as we were zipping up the tent sides, a lady came over and asked if she could go inside to look. She ended up buying $160 worth of my photos. I did okay for the show total and came out a little ahead after all expenses. Sales-wise, it turned out to be a medium-end average show. I was more than a little disappointed.

I have been doing art shows for twenty-five years now and had been thinking that this might be my last season. It's very hard on whoever is helping me, and it's hard on me physically and mentally, especially when I'm worrying about storms. I was also getting very down about people's apparent lack of interest in what is so important to me, nature. Cityscapes and ballpark photos sell well all the time, but not always nature.

They say that when one door closes, the Lord opens another door. I was thinking that maybe this photography for the state, DHS, might be that other door. Let's face it, traveling a short distance to take some photos is a lot easier and less stressful than sitting all day in the heat or rain trying to sell some photos after paying some very high entry fees at an art show. The Monday morning after the show, I got a call from my contact at DHS, and after apologizing for the short notice, he asked if I was available on June 19 and 20. I was, so on Thursday the nineteenth, they sent me downtown to the Access Living headquarters, downtown Chicago to photograph a seminar called Tickets to Work. There were a few speakers coming in from the Social Security Bureau and a few other speakers. I took seventy-eight photos of the speakers and the viewers. I actually enjoyed myself quite a bit. On Friday, they sent me down to the Rehabilitation and Education Center on West Roosevelt Road to photograph a workshop on people who are becoming traumatic brain injured or spinal cord injured by street and or gang violence. I was to just shoot random photos on whoever attended the workshop. I enjoyed myself equally as much as the day before and shot another sixty-four photos.

I had a one-day six-hour show in Mount Prospect scheduled for Saturday the twenty-first. All week long, the weatherman had been predicting rain for Saturday. When praying before a show, I usually prayed for good weather and good sales. This time, I prayed and asked the Lord if this state photography was the "other door" everyone talks about, and was I supposed to quit doing the shows? On Saturday morning, I was in my wheelchair by 5:00 a.m. I went outside, and the sky was perfectly clear blue and almost no breeze at all, a perfect day for an outside art show and blues fest. We left and got to Mount Prospect to set up. As Karen and Bea, my other part time caregiver, who came along for this show, were hanging the last framed photos, I looked at the sky and couldn't believe it: the sky was as black as night as far as the eye could see in any direction. Then it started to rain. I got into the tent, thinking that this was definitely going to be my last year doing shows. Karen and Bea zipped the sides up on the tent and were talking, and I dozed off for about twenty minutes

I awoke to the sound of the tent being unzipped. It had stopped raining, so I went outside to look at the sky. It was perfectly clear again, not a cloud in the sky. The show was going along okay, and around 2:30 p.m., with ninety minutes still to go, I was down just a little from last year's sales.

A man and his daughter came to my booth and were looking at the framed photos as we talked. He told me he was having his basement redone with all new walls, new ceiling, and track lighting. His daughter picked out an eleven-by-fourteen framed cardinal, and Michael picked out my eagle landing triple. Then he picked out two sixteen-by-twenty unframed prints. I was happy, but he was not finished by a long shot. Michael was still looking, this time at my big twenty-by-twenty-four framed prints. After looking and talking a little bit, he picked out my Mount McKinley shot, and then he picked my shot of two grizzlies fishing the Brooks Falls with a salmon attempting to jump the falls; then he took down my lupine quartet and my "Vigilance" (both wolf shots). When I totaled up the photos the total came to $1,140. This is by far the biggest sale I have ever made. The Lord knows that I have trouble hearing His answers, so this time He made it loud and clear by hitting me over the head with His answer. I am not to quit doing the art shows. People do still care about nature; it just takes the right people. When Michael and I were talking, I had told him about two photos that I had at home, a framed twenty-by-thirty shot with at least seventy eagles in it and my twenty-six-by-thirty-six framed "Two-Bear Katmai Sunrise," and he said that he would like to see them sometime.

I called Michael up on Sunday to thank him profusely and to check to see that all the photos were all right. He said that he and his daughter were just on their way out. They asked if they could came over to see the photos we had talked about. I said that would be great. To cut to the chase, Michael loved my sixteen-by-twenty eagles in a Sitka spruce shot with about twenty eagles perched in a Sitka spruce, but they would like it in a wood frame instead of the aluminum frame. I showed him the frames that I had built that were hanging in my matt cutting room. He picked out a frame that I built last year of a heavy ornate carved wood molding. We switched the frames, and he loved the results. He and his daughter had decided to take the twnety-by-thirty many-eagle shot in the aluminum frame I had it in. Then Michael saw my big twenty-six-by-thirty-six "Two-Bear Katmai Sunrise" shot that I had put into a wood frame build of the same heavy ornate wood. He said that he would take it and the eagles in the Sitka spruce shots that day, and while I was at it, he asked if I could build a wood frame for the twenty-by-thirty many-eagle shot. I found a very nice ash moulding, with a golden finish in my garage and built the frame with that molding. He picked it up last Saturday, bringing his total sale up to $1,850. My feet still have not touched the ground. I know this can't go on forever, but once is enough to give me my answer.

Thank you, Lord.

And a big amen.

TBI (TRAUMATIC BRAIN INJURY) SURVIVORS, 2008

I just celebrated my fifty-fifth birthday. I sure never dreamed that I could live, or wanted to live, this long especially right after my discharge from RIC on August 24, 1982. My accident was on September 8, 1981. If you figure it out, I spent exactly 350 days in the hospital, seven weeks in a deep coma, and then six more weeks in a semicoma. I was given less than a 10 percent chance of surviving the first night. My back was broken, T10- T11 fracture dislocation, causing a lesion of the spine, paralyzing my right leg. My rib cage was all busted up, my collarbone on the right side was broken, and there was a hairline fracture at the C6 vertebra. My cheekbone on the right side was shattered, and the right side of my skull was crushed. I guess I was one of the lucky ones because *other than all that, I didn't even get hurt*. My traumatic brain injury had and still has quite a grip on my life.

I am completely deaf in my right ear from cranial nerve damage, my right eye is almost nonfunctional due to the cranial nerve damage. I am completely paralyzed on the left side, and on top of all that, I'm still just as crazy as I was before my accident. I really meant it when I said that I was one of the lucky ones because my reasoning and cognitive thinking were not really affected by my TBI, at least not after the initial shock wore off.

Everybody who acquires a disability pretty much undergoes the same six stages of death. Denial, anger, bargaining, frustration, depression, and acceptance. I never really went through the denial stage. Once I was fully out of the coma and fully aware of what had happened, there was no chance of denying it. Getting through the periods of depression are a little difficult. Everyone will be different. I was lucky again, in that a simple photograph got me through my periods of depression. It is a photograph of a bull moose grazing in a shallow lake surrounded by towering mountains. I took the photograph one year before my accident. Just looking at the photograph hanging on my wall invoked such a desire to get back to the beautiful area where I took the photograph; it gave me the will to keep going. I wish there was something more encouraging that I could say to everyone out there who is living and dealing with TBI or who knows someone who is dealing with a TBI, but there isn't. Every TBI is different from the next one, and even if the injuries are almost identical, each person will handle their injuries and the aftereffects differently. I will say that if you can survive long enough, things do get better. Your brain will transfer some thought and function processes to other parts of the brain that is not injured—some, but not all. I can now move my left leg and arm a little, but nothing functional. But anything is better than it was. Nothing short of a miracle will give me back the use of my arm or legs, but you can't win them all .

Like many others before me, I have learned to live in a wheelchair and learned to depend on others for the everyday help that I need. And most important of all, I have learned to depend and trust in the Lord to put the right people in my life to help me.

You cannot give up, because the Lord does not put anything in our lives that He doesn't know we can handle. I was angry at the Lord for a long time because of my accident. One night while reading the first book of Kings, it hit me, and I felt that I knew the reason for my accident. In fact I awoke the next morning thanking God for my accident and for my surviving it. My accident wasn't a punishment as I had thought for many years; it was a wake-up call. I now look at my survival as a gift, a second chance at life.

As survivors, you must find your niche in life and go for it. My niche was and still is nature photography. I do believe that that is what has helped to keep me alive all these years. Researching, studying, and planning my photography trips to capture some of the world's most elusive critters on film, or as in my case now, on memory cards, and in some very non-accessible areas. Find your niche, pour your heart and soul into it, excel at it, and encourage others to try—that's what keeps you alive inside.

I would be more than happy to talk to anyone about living with TBI or about photography. I'm no medical expert or even a photography expert, but I have picked up a few things over the years.

Because of my hearing problems, e-mail is the best way for me to converse. I can be contacted at

David Farber
raptorfoto@sbcglobal.net
www.naturallyfarberphotos.com

Take care and God Bless

MORE BLESSINGS
RECENT SMALL PHOTO
ADVENTURES

This past weekend, I was exhibiting my work in what should have been an excellent fine arts show. The show was a terrible disappointment with very little patron traffic.

The weather on Saturday was maybe just a little to perfect, so people who might have visited an art show were busy with other things. On Sunday, a cold front had passed, bringing cold, wet weather. I did not even come close to recouping my entry fee. To say the least, I was a bit down in the dumps because I had really looked forward to a good fine arts show. Monday was a perfect day, weather-wise, so I decided to do the one thing that might bring my spirits up—take pictures, instead of trying to sell them.

When Amy returned from dropping her children off at school, we headed to Crabtree Nature Center, where I had not really gone very much in the last five years or so because of deteriorating upkeep of the trails. All I really planned to do was photograph the Canadian geese and goslings. I easily found one family and photographed it for a few minutes, but the goslings were already much bigger than I had hoped for, so I moved on in search of other prey. I soon came across another favorite subject, a chipmunk, so I worked with him for a while getting a few good shots. Amy came over and told me she had seen an eastern bluebird perched on a tree stump behind the Nature Center building near to where there was a bluebird nesting box. In nearly thirty-eight years of photography, I have never gotten a good photograph of an eastern bluebird, so I immediately abandoned my chipmunk and went off in search of a bluebird. The nesting box is located in a field about sixty feet off a cement patio in back of the Nature Center building. I positioned myself so that I could watch the tree stump where Amy had seen the bluebird, the nest box, and surrounding trees without too much movement.

After about a half hour, I spotted the male bluebird about sixty feet away high up on a branch of an old oak tree not to far from the patio. I managed to get off four shots before he took off. I was using my new 10.2 megapixel camera, so I wasn't worried about the distance because I knew that I could do some cropping to enlarge the image without losing any quality. I was elated to have gotten some shots, and I thanked the Lord for helping me point my camera in the right direction. The goose/gosling shots were okay, a few of the chipmunk shots were good enough to work with for art shows, and the bluebird shots were far better than any shots I had ever gotten, definitely workable and saleable. I couldn't wait to work with them. I was so excited about the bluebird shots that I decided to go back there on Tuesday morning. We got there about an hour before the Nature Center opened. Amy got me hooked up with my utility frame and camera then left to get her kids off to school. When the gates opened at 8:00 a.m., I rolled up to the Nature Center and took up position on the patio to look for the bluebird. I had been sitting there for about forty-five minutes without more than a passing glimpse of the bluebird.

Another photographer, Alan, came around the Nature Center building and set up his tripod and camera on the patio near me, and we talked for a few minutes. Alan then did something that I had heard about but had never seen in action. He walked over to a dead tree at the edge of the patio, only about twenty feet away from where we were sitting, and placed an MP3 player with a small speaker system on the ground next to the tree. On this MP3 player, he had recordings of bluebird and other bird songs. I couldn't believe it; within minutes both the male and female bluebirds were in the tree. On Monday, when I had gotten the few shots of the bluebird, he had been up in an old oak tree in shadow from the leaves. Now both bluebirds were in bright sunshine only twenty feet away. We had a good time talking while we shot, and over the next fifteen minutes or so, I shot well over 130 bluebird shots including a few of the pair sitting only inches apart. Alan had been a real godsend.

After Alan left, Amy and her youngest daughter, Jackie, got there and we went out on the trail for a walk. We decided to walk the short trail to see what there was to see. I had to take it real slow and easy because the trail is very overgrown, and last time I was there about five years ago, I had hit a rut, and my wheelchair had tipped over. As we neared the far end of the pond, we spotted a green heron. This was another species that I had never had any luck in photographing. He was standing on a log in bright sunshine just posing for me about seventy feet away, so I shot him many times. Soon enough, a woman and her very noisy young son came down the trail and spooked the heron, but even this turned out to be a blessing. He flew only a short distance, parallel to the shore, before landing on another log and again posed for me. At the end of this log was a short branch sticking up at an angle. The heron walked over and put one foot up on the branch—great pose. Then he put the other foot on the branch and leaned out over the water, an even better pose with great photographic possibilities. After I had more than enough photographs, he again took off, but this time disappeared from the area. It was almost time to go home anyway. What a wonderful day. The Lord knew just what I needed to lift my spirits.

We didn't really see much else, so I finished up the morning with a few shots of Jackie and a couple of bullfrog portraits. What a completely amazing morning, and all before eleven o'clock in the morning. Since I got so many great shots, I have been able to be ruthlessly picky, and after eliminating any shot that did not look just right, I still have sixty-eight excellent bluebird shots left—many close full profile and many close full frontal shots. After eliminating the few where I had chopped off someone's head, I still have four great pair shots with the male and female only inches apart, both perched sitting full profile. Thank you, Lord.

My blessings continued, and in July, when my friends Cindy and Gary invited Amy and I to come up to their place just outside Minocqua, Wisconsin. The loons had successfully nested this year on Middle Ellerson Lake, where their property was located. On a virtually flawless July 20, Amy and I drove the 315 miles up to Minocqua. We stayed in town, and very early the next morning, which was equally as flawless as the day before, we drove out to Cindy and Gary's place. Gary maneuvered his pontoon barge as close to the very muddy shore as possible, and we managed to get my lift and my ramps positioned as a bridge between my van and the barge, and I rolled onto the barge. We spent the next three hours photographing two adult and two loon chicks. After the first hour or so, they got used to us and swam as close as fifteen feet away from the barge. I shot 350 loon family photos that morning.

What great fun, plus I got some great shots of individual loons, loon pair shots, chicks alone, and great family shots.

In August, after I learned that my van needed about $2000 worth of work done, I was a little down in spirits. When we got home, I went into my room and looked out the window, and again, the Lord knew just what I needed. On my hummingbird feeder was a male ruby-throated hummingbird. In the twenty-six years that I have lived in this house, I have never seen a male Ruby-throated hummingbird at my feeder. I have my camera mounted on a unit right at my window so that I can photograph the birds that come to any of my six birdfeeders. My hummingbird feeder is only about eight feet away from my window, and I had my 400 mm zoom lens mounted to my camera. I keep the window very clean so that I can shoot right through the window without opening it. Over the next three weeks, I shot almost seven hundred photos of both the male and female ruby-throated hummingbirds.

How I love this digital camera. It gives me so much more freedom than my old film cameras used to because I don't have to worry about what every shot will cost me.

I used to shoot only slide film. A roll of 36 exposures cost about 6.00 per roll, add to that another 9.00 per roll developing cost. Even doing all my own printing it still cost me a minimum of 15.00 per roll. The loon shoot would have cost me about 150.00, and now this hummingbird would have cost me another 300.00. Knowing that taking so many photos will cost so much money kind of takes some of the enjoyment out of it. Now I can shoot for the fun of it, download the photos and reuse the memory card without it costing me anything except a little time and electricity.

AFRICA, A LIFETIME DREAM

HOW THE DREAM BEGAN

I guess I've always been somewhat of a dreamer. My dreams have never been of great riches or a life of luxury. They have always been about wildlife and the natural world we live in. At about the age of four or five, after seeing my first *Tarzan* or *Bomba, the Jungle Boy* show on TV, I always dreamed or fantasized about a life like that, roaming the jungles of Africa, living with the animals, that sort of thing. During my teenage years and early twenties while I was doing my studies with venomous snakes, I dreamed of traveling to Africa to catch snakes and also to photograph the African wildlife. I can't help it; I just want to live around and with critters. It doesn't matter how big or dangerous they are, I just don't seem to have any fear of them. I have great respect for their speed and power, but I have absolutely no fear of any critter or what it can or may do to me. If it happens, it happens. Since I gave my life over to our Lord in 2003, I seem to have even less of a worry about what can happen. I guess I figure if the Lord wants me to get mauled or eaten by a critter of some kind, then that is the way it is going to be, and nothing I can do will change or prevent that from happening. The inverse of that is also true. If the Lord doesn't want me to be harmed by any critter, no matter how big or small, then no critter will harm me. Life is much simpler when you learn to walk—or in my case, roll—with the Lord. Put your trust in Jesus, and He will see you through anything and everything.

My greatest thrill and enjoyment so far was when, in 2004, I finally made it up to the Katmai National Park at the base of the Aleutian Islands in Alaska to be close to and photograph the great Alaskan coastal brown bears (grizzlies) in the wild. I received the same enjoyment when, in 2007, I traveled to the edge of the Arctic in Churchill, Canada, to photograph polar bears in the wild. Dreams come true. Since my accident in 1981, my Africa dreams were pretty much trashed. In my mind, that sort of a trip is impossible. I can't go to Africa on a safari, in a wheelchair. It's impossible.

Nothing is impossible for the Lord. In December 2008, I went to a travel expo to say hello to the people from Churchill, who had a booth there. I wanted to show them some of the polar bear photos that I had gotten there and give them some of my DVDs to give out to everyone who helped when I was up there. While at the expo, something prompted me to stop at a travel Africa booth, just to tickle my dream.

About ten days later, I received a call from the travel Africa people. They told me about a husband and wife team, Mike and Silvia Hill, in South Africa who run a safari company, Endeavour Safaris, that specializes in senior and disability Safaris (check out this amazing website www.endeavour-safaris.com).

The moment I received this news, I knew that, God willing, somehow, I had to make the trip.

I have prayed about this trip every day since receiving the news and have asked, "Lord, if this Africa trip is not something that You want me to do, please take it away from me. If it is what

You want me to do, please, Lord, I need Your help getting there. And Lord I need Your help with the physical strength to spend at least thirty hours each way on a plane."

After some e-mailing to Mike and Silvia Hill, it seems that the very best place in all Africa for what I want is in September, in Botswana, in the northwest area of the Kalahari Desert. The great Okavango River travels 2,500 miles down through the Angolan Highlands and just spills into this area of the Kalahari Desert, creating the Okavango Delta, the largest inland delta in the world, some six thousand plus-square-mile delta of fast moving crystal clear waters, mopane forests, vast grasslands, and islands. The waters are teeming with fish, Nile crocodiles, hippos, and wading birds. The biodiversity of the area is 164 species of mammals, 157 species of reptiles, 38 species of amphibians, 80 species of fish, and over 500 species of birds.

The grasslands attract many species of antelope and gazelle, zebras, giraffes, and elephants. These grazing species attract lions, leopards, cheetahs, and many other smaller predators.

In 1964, the northeastern one thousand square miles of the Okavango Delta was designated the Moremi Game Reserve. And this area is where, God willing, I will be spending six days and nights.

The more I pray about this trip, the more I feel that this is what the Lord wants me to do. As of right now, God willing, the trip is scheduled for ten days, departing on September 04, 2010. This is hopefully the Itinerary for the trip.

2010 AFRICAN SAFARI UPDATE

The original plan was to have flown on South African Air nonstop to Johannesburg, South Africa. We stay overnight there, and the next morning we were to have flown from Johannesburg to Maun, Botswana on Botswana air. That was the plan since the conception of this trip back in January 2009.

In September 2009, with just under a year to go, we were informed by Botswana Air that due to the reduced cargo space in their new planes, they were not going to allow me to bring my electric wheelchair on the plane. Endeavour Safaris talked to everyone they could in Botswana and South Africa. The travel people up here talked to everybody they could, all to no avail. Botswana Air adamantly refused to allow my chair on board with the excuse that it would take up to much space in the cargo hold. I had even contacted the North American sales manager for Botswana Air.

Endeavour Safari and I immediately started to work on alternate routes and plans to try to get us up to the Moremi Game Reserve. One plan was to fly on South Africa Air up to Livingstone in Zambia near Victoria Falls and drive back to the Moremi from there, adding two days to the trip. After the safari, we would fly back from Maun to Johannesburg via charter flight. I loved this idea because we would drive through the Chobe game reserve on the way giving us more photo ops. Unfortunately the cost of the charter plane was quite astronomical, raising the overall cost of the safari by over $1,000 per person, plus another 1,500 per person for the extra days. Total cost of the safari including international airfare jumped to well over $6000 per person.

I was heartbroken but not quite ready to admit defeat on the whole safari idea.

With Botswana out, I reformulated plans to just stay in South Africa and go on a safari to the Kruger National Park. Things were going great, the quotes were good, and Endeavour Safari said that they were working on getting an accessible open vehicle for use in South Africa and in Kruger. I was ready to book the trip.

About December 10, I received the e-mail from Endeavour Safaris telling me that the open vehicle would not be ready in time for our September safari.

I cannot sit in a closed van and expect to get professional quality photos through auto glass. I can barely see out of my van windows even when they are sparkling clean because I sit so high in my chair and my poor vision. Besides, if I wanted to shoot photos through a closed window, I might as well just go to the zoo. It would be much easier and even cheaper. I told Silvia that we would just have to wait another year until the open accessible vehicle was ready.

Silvia at Endeavour Safaris said that was why they had wanted to get me to Botswana in the first place and then suggested the possibility of driving all the way from Johannesburg to Maun and back, but this would add four days to the safari. I asked her to send me a quote and a proposed itinerary even though I figured that it would be just too much more expensive.

I was out of ideas and totally defeated, also very confused. We have been studying the book *Living Waters* by Chuck Smith. I just read about gifts of the Holy Spirit. First He puts the idea into our heart, then into our mind. Why would He put this idea into my heart and mind only to have it fail so completely everywhere we turned? I had been praying about this trip since the very beginning. I let myself get very depressed; my lifetime dream looked as though it was going to be just that, a dream, not a reality.

On December 16, 2009, I received an e-mail from the North American sales manager of Botswana Air telling me that everything was clear if I wanted to go ahead and book the flights with him, both international flights and the flight from Johannesburg to Maun.

I had been warned not to trust him, that he was just interested in selling us tickets and we might just get to Johannesburg and be left sitting on the tarmac because there is no room on the plane.

I prayed even more that night because I just didn't know if I should trust him or not. What did the Lord want me to do?

The next morning, December 17, just eight days before Christmas, I woke up and I had an e-mail from Endeavour Safaris. It was the quote and proposed itinerary for driving all the way from Johannesburg to Maun, the six-day safari into the Moremi Game Reserve and then driving back to Johannesburg. Not only do I get to spend four days traveling by Mercedes van across the magnificent Kalahari Desert, the whole trip comes out just a little more expensive for me, but a $140 less per person for everyone else. My cost was slightly higher because the lodge in Francistown cannot accommodate three people in a room, so I had to be booked into a single rather than sharing with Amy and Jackie.

I know. "Oh ye of so little faith." Now I know why the original plans failed.

Even though I had said, "If the Lord wanted me to get there, then He was going to get me there." I was unwilling to give up trying to control the trip. Even when I was ready to settle for less than the Moremi Game Reserve by staying in South Africa's Kruger National Park, it didn't work. It wasn't until I gave up trying to control the trip and said, "Okay, we will just have to wait another year until the accessible vehicle is ready for Kruger," that the Lord took over and showed me what He could do. Now I get to experience up close the magnificent beauty of the Kalahari Desert. The Lord wanted me to get the most out of the experience I've dreamed of since I was four years old.

BOTSWANA SAFARI FINAL COUNTDOWN

Fifty-three years of dreaming

September 08, 1981 my accident
Almost twenty-nine years since I gave up my dreams of Africa because in my mind it was an impossible dream.

Twenty-one months since December '08, when the Lord showed me that Africa in a wheelchair is possible and He dropped this trip in my lap. I immediately took over the planning of this gift from the Lord.

September '09, eleven months ago when the trip fell apart because Botswana air refused to allow my electric wheelchair on board the plane.

October '09 the alternate plan that I figured out failed.

December '09 the second alternate plan of a simpler trip I planned failed and I finally gave up my hopes of Africa.

December 18, '09 in the blink of an eye the Lord fixes everything and comes up with a trip the likes of which that I never would have planned for myself, two days traveling across the Kalahari, six days in the Moremi Game Reserve and two days traveling back across the Kalahari.

August 29, 2010 we are now down to just 135 hours until we leave for O'hare airport on this very blessed trip.

I look forward to sharing the whole trip with everyone after Sept 17, 2010

God Bless

LIVING WITH A TBI
(TRAUMATIC BRAIN INJURY)

On August 8, 2009, I will be fifty-six years old. On August 24, 2009, I will be celebrating the twenty-seventh year of my discharge from the Rehabilitation Institute of Chicago. Just fifteen days later, on September 8, 2009, I will celebrate (although very quietly) the twenty-eighth anniversary of my accident. Most people might wonder why I celebrate something as horrific as an accident that almost killed me and left me completely paralyzed except for my right arm? I celebrate, first of all because, for one thing, I am still here to celebrate, and the best reason to celebrate is because the Lord is not done with me yet. He still has things for me to do here to glorify Him.

Yes, the simple wildlife photography that I do glorifies Him because He created everything I love to photograph. He gave me the love I have of nature, and He gave me the talent and abilities that I have to do the photography. It took me a long time to learn this. I didn't come by this talent by my hard work or by some fluke of nature, but by the gifts of the Holy Spirit.

For a very long time after my accident, I was angry at the Lord for allowing this to happen to me, and for a time I looked at my accident as punishment for the ungodly way that I lived most of my life, that is, until I realized that if it were punishment it would have been much worse. Now that my eyes are open, I view my accident as a gift, a second chance at life to do things the right way by following the Lord. When I finally started reading the Bible in 2002, this verse helped me to see things more clearly:

> "For I know the plans I have for you," declares the Lord, "plans to prosper you and not to harm you, plans to give you hope and a future."
>
> —Jeremiah 29:11

It seems clear-cut that this verse is telling me that the Lord has plans for you no matter what your situation in life. In order for the Lord to carry out His plans for your life you must first submit to Him and learn to be led by the Holy Spirit.

I'm still learning this, but I tend to rush into things headlong, and then I end up sitting there praying that the Lord will fix everything that I just messed up.

Just learn to trust in the Lord and He will get you through your troubles. You may be quite surprised at what the Lord has planned for your life, I certainly have been.

If somebody would have told me, almost 30 years ago, that I would travel to Alaska, to some of the most remote inaccessible regions, to the very edge of the Arctic, and now to Africa in a wheelchair, I would have thought they were crazy. But ever since I accepted Jesus Christ into my life as my Personal Lord and Savior things have been quite amazing.

Traumatic brain injuries can take years before they start to heal. Before any healing can really begin, your attitude must be right. Walking or rolling with the Lord will give you that right attitude. But remember that the Lord's time frame is not the same as our time frame so things may move slower than you want, but when the Lord decides that the time is right and they do move, you will be surprised at the outcome.

A friends' pastor gave this benediction last Sunday:

> Wherever you go, God is sending you, wherever you are, God has put you there; He has a purpose in your being there. Christ who indwells you has something He wants to do through you where you are. Believe this and go in His grace and love and power.

THE ADVENTURE BEGINS

I was dressed and ready to go by 5:00 a.m. Amy and Jackie arrived at about 5:30. The van was already packed and ready to go. Everything was checked and rechecked. Jimmy, my friend who was driving us to the airport, arrived at 6:00 a.m.

Well! The Lord got us safely, although not totally without a little delay and misadventure, to our destination in Johannesburg, South Africa. By a little delay, I mean an hour or so delay in departing from Dulles International Airport in Washington and then the two-hour delay in Dakar, Senegal, for refueling and flight crew change.

My wheelchair should be waiting for me when I get off the plane. The first misadventure was when we got to Dulles International in Washington DC. My electric chair was nowhere to be found; for two hours I was stuck in that unpadded narrow aisle chair wondering where the heck my chair was and thinking that this was not a good way to start the adventure of my life. They finally found my chair sitting unattended by the freight elevator. It seems someone forgot to bring it up so they just left it there. It was not just my wheelchair that I was worried about. My custom-made one-of-a-kind utility frame that I use to hold my camera when I am doing my photography was firmly strapped to the back frame of the wheelchair. Luckily everything was fine, nothing broken or lost this time.

09-05-10

We finally made it to Johannesburg where misadventure number two hit. Again they "lost" my wheelchair, but this time, when the chair was found, they had for some reason cut the heavy strapping that held my utility frame, packed in a heavy duty army duffle bag to the frame of the chair, and of course lost my utility frame. There was no reason at all that the utility frame had to be touched. Why did they cut it off my chair?

I was more than just a little upset and angry enough, that I was ready to get back on a plane and go home because there is no way that I could do my photography without that frame.

Finally, after almost another three hours of not finding the frame, I was off in a corner by myself praying. This time, instead of just praying that someone find my frame, I prayed, "Lord, You know where my utility frame is. You know where everything is. Nothing is hidden from Your eyes. Please turn somebody's eyes to my utility frame." It wasn't two minutes later that Jackie, Amy's daughter, came running up to me and said, "We found it." The relief was so great and immediate that tears of gratitude to the Lord were flowing from my eyes to the point that I couldn't see straight.

Silvia at Endeavour Safaris, unknown to us, had booked us into a beautiful luxury casino hotel just twenty minutes from the airport. When we got there at about 9:00 p.m., after sitting for over thirty-six straight hours, I just collapsed into bed until about four fifteen the next morning.

09-06-10

After a beautiful buffet breakfast, included with the room, we were ready to go.

We were picked up at 7:00 a.m., ready to start the first leg of our journey, a 375-mile drive through the northeast part of South Africa, over the Botswana border and up to Francistown, where we were to stay overnight. Unfortunately, the hotel in Francistown messed up the reservations. Amy, Jackie, and I were supposed to have adjoining suites on the first floor, but they had booked Amy and Jackie into a room on the second floor—no elevators and no working phones. Audrey and Cecily, both seniors with difficulty walking, were also supposed to have a first-floor room, but were also booked into 2nd floor rooms and Cecily had a slight mishap climbing the stairs, luckily she was not hurt very badly, just bruised and angry.

None of us was very happy about the mess-up. They were finally able to bring in an extra mattress, so Amy and Jackie shared the mattress on the floor. We all made it through the night.

09-07-10

We left on the second leg of the journey, a 325-mile drive west across the Kalahari to Maun where we would again overnight.

I was not rigged in my utility frame during the whole drive due to the limited room inside the Mercedes Sprinter. I was going to try to use a simple monopod if a photo opportunity should arise, but I'm afraid that the Africa of my dreams was not to be found in the populated regions unless I wanted to photograph herds of mules or goats or flocks of chickens. By the time we got to Maun, I hoped never to see another mule or goat again. We did see one bateleur eagle, but I was not fast enough at maneuvering in the sprinter to get a shot out the small opening of the windows. With the Lord's help, I did get a few nice shots of a steenbok, a very small large-eared antelope species, who posed for me before disappearing in the blink of an eye. Also with the Lord's help, I got my first shots of a wild ostrich during that drive. We arrived at Maun in good time and stayed at a very nice safari lodge on the Thalamakane, pronounced Tha la ma Ka nee River.

We had beautiful private chalets, each with a little outside built in wading pool which Jackie made use of. I immediately, with Amy's help, got set up in my utility frame and started taking photos of the exotic looking birds and beautiful river sunset. We all had dinner at around 8:00 pm.

09-08-10

Today is the twenty-ninth anniversary of my accident, and I can't believe how blessed I am to be spending it this way, doing something that I have dreamed about since I was four years old.

After a good night's sleep and an early breakfast, we set off on our final drive of a hundred kilometers (just over sixty miles) north up to the South Gate of the Moremi Game Preserve. After about the first hour, we were finally away from the last of the little suburban villages with all their goats, mules, and chickens. I was hoping to see real wild critters, and I finally realized that the Africa in my dreams came from watching TV all my life. That sixty-minute documentary showing tons of animal species all crammed together was not only a Hollywood Africa, but the sixty minutes of TV probably took two to three hundred hours of filming.

Don't get me wrong, we did see tons of critters just not as soon as I was hoping for. When we got near the south gate entrance to the Moremi Game Reserve, 1,200 square miles of open, no fences at all, delta area, hopes were high for wildlife sightings. The first critter we saw was a lone giraffe grazing on leaves just fifty or so feet away, amazing in the wild. Very shortly after the giraffe we came across a troop of vervet monkeys, and I was having a ball taking photos. We drove on stopping whenever we saw various critters, mostly different antelope species.

We came to a clearing where we pulled off the trail to break for a picnic lunch. About fifty yards away, there was a small group of about six red lechwe (another antelope species). I was not hungry and decided to try to get a few shots of the lechwe and the termite mounds in the area. Mike didn't want me wandering off by myself because of the dangers, so I didn't go very far. With the Lord's help I did get a few shots of the Lechwe that are usable.

I'm glad I did because we didn't see any more the rest of the safari. After the lunch break we pushed on towards our campsite area on the Xakanaxa Lagoon. We came across a lone elephant grazing on the foliage in a clearing. I got a few photos before we moved on. It was the hottest part of the day and nothing was moving very much. Mike got a call over the radio from another safari driver from another outfit telling him about a lion sighting on the way to the Xakanaxa, pronounced simply kanaka.

We came across the small lion pride during the very hottest (about 87 degrees) but very dry air. The male lion was fast asleep under some bush, but a couple of the females were up and about. With the Lord's help, I was able to get a few shots of female lions before they moved at an angle where I could no longer shoot. This was a problem that plagued me the entire trip. The drivable trails were so bumpy and winding my wheelchair had to be very tightly secured to the floor allowing me no chair movement at all, and still it was all I could do to hold on so that I wouldn't be thrown forward in my seat and eat my camera that is always mounted in front of me for immediate access.

I thought that it was very rough when I was up in the Wapusk National Park in 2007 photographing the polar bears where the only smooth spots on the trails was when the tundra buggy was balanced on top of a boulder for a few seconds before it came crashing down. The trails here didn't even have the boulders to balance on; it was that rough, and I hadn't imagined that it would be that rough, making shooting photographs except when completely stopped impossible. Of course, with my very limited mobility and vision, just seeing the critters was a constant problem. Mike always tried to maneuver the large Toyota Landcruiser around so that everyone could get a look or photos of everything but sometimes the terrain just didn't allow for much maneuvering of the vehicle. More than a few times, I completely missed a photo op because the critter or bird was completely on my blind side in a tight area where Mike just couldn't turn the vehicle.

Around 6:00 p.m., Mike pulled up to a large water hole area just surrounded on all sides with dozens and dozens of impalas, waterbucks, and a few other species of antelope plus quite a few species of different birds in and around the water. We stayed there for the first night's sunset around 6:30. It was truly awe-inspiring. Watching and photographing the sunset behind huge herds of impalas and the other antelope species. Very shortly after the sunset, but still light enough out to take photos using available light, we came to a very large clearing with more elephants than I had ever seen in my life. What magnificent creatures when seen in the wild where they belong. This sight completely erased any frustrations that I had had during the day's drive.

This was looking more like the Africa that I had dreamed of. It was also the greatest gift the Lord gave me from the trip. All my life I have seen elephants in zoos, on TV, and even in the circus when I was a kid. I never really appreciated them; they were just big elephants that stood around doing nothing. They weren't beautiful by a long shot—I didn't dislike them, they were just there. Here in the wild, I couldn't get enough of them. Thank you, Lord, for opening my eyes, again, to the real beauty of the largest of all Your land creatures on the face of this planet. The thrill of seeing the elephants reacting to each other and grouping together as family units was something I will remember until the day I die.

We drove the rest of the way to the camp in darkness except for the headlights. We had a light dinner that Friday the camp chef had prepared and retired to our designated tents for the night's sleep on camp cots under thick warm comforters. There was no electricity in the tents so the only light came from a small led lamp that I had brought with, and that was very insufficient, but we made do.

09-09-10

With all the excitement of everything we saw yesterday afternoon and evening when we first entered the Moremi Game Reserve, and after only two to three hours sleep, I didn't think that night would ever end. This day would be our first full day of game drives. I have no idea what Mike has planned today or what the Lord has in store for us, but I'm far too excited to even think about sleeping. I can't see a thing because it's pitch black inside this tent and probably just as dark outside. The only sounds that I think I hear is the crackling of the campfire outside and the imagined ticking of the clock that always seems to be going in my mind. I'm just laying here waiting to hear the sounds of the camp crew starting to move around outside so that I can awaken Amy to help me get up into my chair.

The camp crew starts waking everyone up by 5:30. It's darn cold out here but it will heat up quickly when the sun rises completely.

The crew had a small breakfast table all set up with hot coffee, milk, coco, some fresh hot bread, and dry cereals.

The clock read 7:15 a.m., and we were finally getting underway. The first thing I noticed this morning was that with the first light came an utter cacophony of loud bird calls from everywhere. Even with my limited hearing ability, it seemed very loud, and I loved it. No sounds of traffic or humanity, just pure nature.

The trail we were following out of camp was very winding. As we round yet another sharp curve, just off to our left was a small family group of three or four elephants grazing in a small wooded clearing. Just my luck and another frustrating episode, because today Mike asked me to try facing forward instead of out to the left of the Land Cruiser like I was yesterday. Apparently this made it easier for Doris, who is seated in the wheelchair to my right behind the driver's seat, to see. Doris also has great mobility problems. We were so close to this group of elephants that Mike had no room whatsoever to maneuver the big Land

Cruiser, so I could barely turn my head enough to see and was not able to shoot any photos. The young female elephant in the group was very agitated and twice took a few quick steps in our direction in a mock charge, so we didn't stay very long. As we pulled away, Mike said that she was running after us for a short distance, just to make sure we had really gone. We came out of the wooded area into a small floodplain and the first thing I saw was one of the many blacksmith plovers that inhabit the area and with the Lord's help I was able to get a few good photographs. After some more twists and turns, Mike pulled up to a widening in a river that looked almost like a large pond. Mike pointed out to us some hippos barely visible in the water, with only their ears showing. I hardly noticed this first hippo sighting because I was preoccupied with a nearby pied kingfisher that was posing in a bush overhanging the waters edge. I got some good shots of the kingfisher before turning my attention to the hippo ears that, after a few minutes became much more that just ears. My attention was again drawn away from the hippos by a red-billed hornbill on a broken off tree stump overhanging the water. He was a beautiful, but strange-looking bird, like nothing we have back home in the United States.

I was fascinated by this bird, and with the Lord's help, was able to get some wonderful shots. We probably spent about twenty-five minutes there, watching the birds and hippos before pushing on. The next thing we came across was a lone giraffe in a floodplain area dotted with small trees and bushes. We watched and photographed this giraffe for a few minutes, before again moving on. It wasn't very long before we rounded another bend, all the while looking and hoping to see predators like lions or other big cats. This time we came across another critter that I had really wanted to photograph, a medium-sized herd of plains zebras.

There were probably ten or twelve in the herd with at least two or three mares with foals. They were spread out around and in between the many bushes in the area. The zebras in the zoos were just not the same. I never dreamed they were so beautiful, and I couldn't and didn't want to stop taking photos. With the Lord guiding me, I got some great mare and foal shots and some excellent stallion shots, with him standing off a little distance away from the herd keeping watch. In the first few shots that I took, there was a lone giraffe far off in the background walking away from the area where the zebras were. The striping on the faces of the mares and foals are so perfect, they are mesmerizing. After we had all had our fill of this zebra herd, we pushed on. We were near the edge of a marshy area, and I just got my first sighting of an African fish eagle up in a tree. The photos are just okay because there are many branches, and it is somewhat far away, and we can't get any closer. Walking in the marsh about twenty-five feet away is an African jacana, a medium-sized wading bird, quite stately with a bright light blue patch on the top of its head. There are a few small- to medium-sized Nile crocodiles on the mudflats of the marsh, more blacksmith plovers, and more red-billed hornbills. This is wonderful; there is so much to see and photograph that is so different from the wildlife back home.

I could be happy here forever or until I run out of memory cards. A duck swimming nearby had a blue-gray bill and was identified as a hottentot teal. He posed nicely for me with a nearly perfect reflection beneath him. It had been so exciting, and it seemed like we just got started, but somehow we used up the entire morning, and it was time to head back to camp for our brunch, and then we will rest for the early afternoon, the hottest part of the day, before heading out on our late afternoon game drive. I shot 298 photographs of a great many types of critters. What a wonderful morning. Thank you, Lord.

We had a delicious brunch, which was prepared by the crew chef, Friday. I don't know how Friday created the dishes he served, and he did it all over a camp stove, a simple box placed over the campfire. He was really quite an amazing chef. It was nice and warm outside, about the mid-eighties, but very dry in spite of the fact that we are in an area of rivers and marshes. It is still part of the Kalahari Desert, so the desert air wisps away any humidity.

During this early part of the afternoon, it is designated as a rest time before we head out on our late afternoon game drive. I was unable to go anywhere by myself because it is supposed to be too dangerous, but mostly because the ground is very sandy and I cannot navigate around and through the sand. After brunch with Amy's help, I had transferred out of my chair by scooting onto my cot to stretch, and had just dozed off when I was awaken by Amy, to let me know that there was a troop of about thirty hamadryas baboons playing on the ground and in the trees right outside the back of the tent. Needless to say that I was back in my chair as fast as possible and, with Amy's help, had the utility frame and camera hooked up in minutes; then I asked a couple of the crew to push me to the back area of the tent so I could shoot photos. This was fantastic—the baboons were all over the place and all around us. There were females with very young infant baboons hanging onto their bellies while the slightly older infant baboons were riding on the backs of their parents or older siblings. I had hoped to get a few good shots of baboons but never dreamed that the Lord would send them right to our tent area. This, plus everything we experienced this morning and yesterday, is the Africa of my dreams.

It's funny. In our men's study group in church, we had been reading and discussing the book *Faith* by Chuck Smith. In the chapter we just read, Chuck talks about taking that step of faith and that some people are afraid to do so because they might just end up in deep Africa, in a tent with spiders crawling on the walls and snakes on the ground. This was right after I returned from this trip, and we all laughed because this was what I had dreamed of my entire life.

The baboon troop decided to go elsewhere to look for food, and it is finally time to get ready to leave on our afternoon game drive. We started out slowly and paused so I could shoot a few photos of a pair of Swainson's francolins, medium-sized birds in the grouse family. After another very short time, Mike again stopped the vehicle to point out a pair of swallow-tailed bee-eaters, which are small, very colorful birds, sitting on a branch about fifty feet away. I had a hard time locating the birds using my 800 mm lens, and by the time I zeroed in on them, one had flown the coop. I did however get some very nice shots of the one that stayed. We moved on after a few minutes and drove for some distance without seeing much except for a few impalas.

Again we are in an area dotted with clumps of acacia trees and brush. As Mike rounds another bend in the trail, we came across a family grouping of giraffes grazing on the brush and trees. We're only about twenty or so yards away, but the giraffes paid us no mind. This was better than I could ever have imagined. There were red-billed oxpeckers all over the backs, necks, and even the heads of the giraffes. These are birds that feed on the parasites and bugs that plague the giraffes, zebras, and even the Cape buffalo. We are parked close enough that I can zoom in and get some portrait work done. These giraffes have got to be the goofiest looking creatures to do portrait work with, especially with the oxpeckers perched on their heads. The giraffes moved on, so we continued on with our drive in search of wildlife.

We soon come across one of the many herds of impalas in the area and stopped for a photo shoot. These impala were so sleek and beautiful. I can see why a car was named after them. Somehow, we managed to burn up most of the afternoon, so we left the impala to graze in peace.

We were driving across an open floodplain, and Mike stopped to point out a coppery-tailed coucal. He was a fairly large, crow-sized bird with colors that even surpassed his name. He was coppery colored with white and black markings. He was posing on a dead tree branch about five or six feet off the ground only about twenty feet away, paying us no attention at all. Lord, what a beautiful bird.

Heading back toward camp, we soon came to another small herd of elephants. I couldn't seem to get enough of these amazing creatures. We watched and photographed them until it was getting dark, so we returned to camp in the dark for a dinner around 8:30 p.m. Again, Friday had prepared a feast that was not very good for my diabetes, but what the heck. That evening after dinner, Amy had a little conference with Mike and Friday about a more reasonable menu for my diabetes.

What a wonderful day it had been. I didn't see any of the big cats that I so hoped to see, but I had a ball and shot well over six hundred photographs that day. Thank you, Lord. Everything was so remarkable when seen in the wild.

Tomorrow, we spend the entire day on a boat outing. It's going to be another sleepless night.

09-10-10

We spent the entire day on a boat on the Xakanaxa Lagoon. I have always loved the peacefulness of boating. It was about a two-hour journey (if we don't stop) from the camp to get to the boat launch. But of course we stopped a lot, and within the first fifteen minutes or so, we stopped to watch a couple giraffes grazing on the foliage. We crossed a floodplain dotted with groupings of impala and waterbucks and stopped near what looked like a very shallow pond, but it was deeper than it looked because this shallow pond had at least three hippopotamus (that we can see) in it. They were completely submerged at times, and at other times, they are at the surface of the water with just their ears showing.

On the bank of the pond, there were also three Nile crocodiles (two about six feet long and one that looks to be about ten to thirteen feet) basking in the sun, waiting for their next meal. There was an African fish eagle perched on a nearby tree and a number of other birds in the surrounding brush and on the ground. After about thirty minutes, we got underway again. Mike got a call over the radio, and he told us about a leopard sighting.

It was about thirty-five minutes out of the way in an area where there is a possibility that we might get stuck. He asked us if we want to try for it, and we all voted yes. The leopard is the most elusive cat in all Africa, and I would love to get a few shots of one.

After passing over more open floodplains and mixed brush veldt, we stopped for a few minutes to watch and photograph a lone bull elephant giving himself a dust bath, and while we were watching the elephant, a black-backed jackal wandered by, and then we were again underway. Traveling from point A to point B in the Moremi Game Reserve was never in a straight line, and you never know what you will see around the next bend or during the next minute, so it was always exciting and very bumpy. We finally came to the area where the leopard was, and found out that there was a National Geographic film truck there. They said that they had been following and filming this leopard for two days now. The leopard was up in a tree, and Mike maneuvered the Land Cruiser into a position where we might be able to see the leopard. I barely got a glimpse (no photographs) of him up in the tree when all of a sudden he jumped down and disappeared into the surrounding brush.

I couldn't be more disappointed; I really wanted to get a few shots of the big cats in the wild. The day was still just getting underway, so all was not lost. We just passed through a small wooded area where we stopped for a few minutes to watch a troop of fifteen to twenty vervet monkeys and a nearby family of three hamadryas baboons.

We finally made it to the boat launch. I looked over the boat to try and figure the best way for Mikes crew to get me into the boat without killing me or anyone else. The boat is about 18 feet long and about 9 feet wide with seating on both sides and a canopy roof for shade. There is an open area in the front just big enough for me to maneuver my chair around in. The front or bow of the boat was beached.

After talking to Mike, I raised my seat as high as possible and scooted onto the very front little bow deck, then four of Mikes' crew picked up my 265 pound chair and lifted it into the boat then they picked me up off the bow deck and placed me back into my chair. Everybody else pretty much climbed in the same way, sitting on the front bow deck and pivoting around into the boat. Doris, a young lady from Switzerland, and the only other person in our group confined to a wheelchair, (a manual chair) was just picked up and carried onto the boat. She and her mother and sister will sit in the seats in the shaded area of the boat.

Once we were all settled, one of Mike's crew pushed us off, and we got underway. Since we spent so much time stopping and detouring to the leopard sighting, Mike was in a hurry to get us to the rookery. The leisurely boat ride that I envisioned turned out to be a somewhat high-speed boat ride down a maze of channels through tall papyrus reeds. After about two hours of twisting and turning through this maze of channels, we finally broke into a large open body of water, which was the rookery. The whole area was surrounded by tall bushes and trees, and every bush and small tree was almost totally covered with nesting storks, egrets, herons, and a myriad of other birds. We spent about ninety minutes cruising around the edge of the rookery where I shot about five hundred photographs of marabou storks, yellow-billed storks, open-billed storks, gray herons, great white egrets, little egrets, sacred ibis, and darters, plus a few that I have not yet even identified. After we left the rookery on the way back to the dock area, we soon pulled up to a small open clearing on shore for a little picnic lunch on the boat.

While we were sitting there, with the front of the boat beached, enjoying our lunch in the perfect peacefulness that comes only when you are out in the wilderness, far from any man-made noise, we heard the snapping of a large branch. At the snapping sound, we looked up, and on top of the embankment not more than, say, fifteen feet away and a good ten feet up, was a large bull elephant enjoying his own lunch of fresh green branches. He was magnificent! I forgot all about lunch and started shooting photographs. The perspective was amazing. On the ground, the elephant would seem very tall. but sitting here on the boat looking up an embankment into the face of an already tall creature, he looked huge. I loved watching this beautiful creature use his trunk to break branches off then stuff them into his mouth with much more manual dexterity than I could get out of my hand. He was flaring his ears in an agitated mode, probably wondering what we were doing in his favorite eating and bathing area. Every time he turned to leave, he would turn back for another look at us. Finally he turned and left, so (with lunch finished) we continue on our own way back to the boat launch.

When we arrived back at the launch, I waited for everyone else to climb off the boat. Then I transfered onto the little bow deck and waited until Mikes' crew lifted my chair off the boat and came back for me. Once I was back in my chair and buckled in everyone climbed back onto the Toyota land cruiser for the two hour + ride back to camp. It was dark by the time we arrived back at camp after numerous stops along the way to look at and photograph different critters. It had been a fantastic day. The Lord has really blessed all of us today with some great shooting sessions.

09-11-10

I had another very restless night because I was just to excited about everything here to waste time sleeping. I was lying on my cot with no idea what time it was because it was still pitch black in the tent. I could hear Amy's and Jackie's breathing from deep under their heavy comforters, it was darn cold out there. Nothing was stirring outside except the occasional crackle of the campfire or the gas lamps that were kept burning low all night long in order to keep any critters away, although I would have welcomed a visit from a lion or a leopard, just to help pass the time. I was trying to imagine what the day would bring and prayed for the Lord to bless us abundantly during the upcoming day's game watching. This will be our third full day in the Moremi Game Reserve. Today we will be moving our campsite area from the Xakanaxa Lagoon to the northern border of the Moremi Game Reserve on the Kwai River. We will also be heading somewhat east. I have no idea how far of a drive it will be, but I do know that the northern area of the Moremi has more floodplain area, which by this time of the year should be drier than the area around the Xakanaxa Lagoon. I finally heard the camp crew moving around outside getting things started. Soon came the wakeup call, so it must be about 5:00 am. It was pretty cold here especially after huddling under a thick down comforter all night. Amy was up by then and helped me into my wheelchair. Jackie was still buried under the warm comforter on her cot. After Amy finished getting ready she helped me get setup in my utility frame and camera. The crew already had a small breakfast table set up with some juice, hot coffee, dry granola cereal and some fresh hot bread that melts in your mouth. . We finally got going with everyone in the land cruiser and the other truck with all the luggage, camp equipment, and tents was up ahead.

We couldn't have been moving more than ten minutes or so when Mike stopped so that I could photograph an immature martial eagle perched on top of a dead tree trunk very close to the trail. It is a very handsome bird, even in its immature plumage. I prayed that I might get the chance to photograph a mature one before the trip is over. A few minutes later, Mike again pulled up to let us watch and photograph a female blacksmith plover huddled in the grasses by the trail protecting her chicks. She was almost too close for me to get any real good shots, but she was fun to watch. It was probably about nine thirty in the morning, and it had warmed up considerably.

Soon we were crossing a large marshy area, and stopped because the truck carrying all the gear was having a little trouble.

While Mike was talking to his crew chief, I was enjoying myself photographing a great egret about seventy-five feet away. Wouldn't you know it, I finally got to photograph my first African frog species, unfortunately, it was sticking out of the end of the Great egrets bill. Brunch, I guess. With the Lord's help, I got a few very nice shots but I was unable to identify the frog species. While we were sitting there, a black-backed jackal wandered by. Amy and Charlotte both got some very nice shots of this very beautiful animal. Unfortunately, by the time he got into a position where I could see him, all I got was the rear-end view.

In a bush nearby was another new species for me to photograph, and this time I was in a good position. It was a yellow-billed hornbill, and with the Lord's help, I was able to get a few nice shots of him. There were a couple of very homely warthogs nearby. Neither one had large tusks, so after a few shots, we got underway again. We soon passed an area with clusters of brush and small trees. Among this brush was another small herd of plains zebras. We have seen zebras three times now, but they are just as beautiful now as they were the first time, and I was able to get some more nice shots. We just broke into a clearing, and there are more zebras, this time mixed in with some blue wildebeests. The wildebeests were very clumsy looking compared to the very sleek zebras with their racing stripes. After a few minutes we got underway again, Amy spotted another lilac-breasted roller perched on a branch of another short dead tree.

This was a perfect photo opportunity. He was only about ten feet or so off the ground, just a little above my height while seated in the Land Cruiser. Mike circled around, and I was able to get my very best full profile shots yet. What a magnificently colored bird. He looks as though he was hand painted by the hand of God. After everybody had their fill of photographing this bird who had posed so perfectly, we got under way again, but not very far because now Mike pointed out an ostrich at the edge of the clearing. After watching and photographing this ostrich for a few minutes, it moved into the dense brush, so we moved on. Scattered among the brush clumps were more small groupings of blue wildebeests and a few scattered impala. We stopped to look at these, but none were clear enough to do much photography. Next we moved into an area where the brush was not as dense, and we spotted more small groupings if plains zebras. These made for better photography opportunities as they stood posing in pairs and trios, some with nice blue water in the background.

As we were watching and photographing these zebras, a hamerkop came strutting by. He is a very strange, but interesting-looking bird. Thank God, it was a good photo op. We broke into a very large expanse of wide open floodplain, and as we came around a curve in the trail, Mike stopped suddenly. About seventy-five yards in front of us, there was a very large herd of water buffalo that stretched almost as far as the eye can see. This was wonderful, what a great photo op. They are all crowded into a large marshy area. Amy, standing up in the Land Cruiser to better photograph the buffalo, asked Mike if these things ever stampeded. Mike's answered, "Yup, do you want me to get a little closer?" After watching these buffalo for a little while, we cautiously moved on and continued towards our destination at the Kwai River campsite.

There was a white-backed vulture perched up in a tree near the trail, and nearby there was a nest in a tree with a saddle-billed stork standing on it. We were taking a short break, so I decided to shoot some photos of the many water lilies in bloom all around.

After we moved on a little ways, Mike spotted a long-tailed shrike standing on top of a somewhat trampled down termite mound. He was another interesting, but not very colorful, bird that was fun to photograph.

The day was barely half over, and the Lord has shown us so many new sights, critters, and interesting birds. There were a few hippos grazing out in the somewhat dry marshy area along with some impalas. There were also a few great egrets wandering around out there, and another African fish eagle perched on a low tree branch about fifty yards away.

We were on the move again and entered another large dry floodplain. Mike pulled to a stop again because up ahead a little ways was a very large bull elephant. He was all alone as bulls tend to be when not mating. This one was in the process of giving himself a good dust bath. It was beautiful, and with the Lord's help, I got some great shots of this elephant with a cloud of dust above his head.

We left the bull elephant behind and continue on our way, pausing only briefly for more zebras and warthogs. Among the brush and trees in this area were a few more small clusters of elephants with impala walking around.

We then entered a very strange-looking, heavily wooded area. There was no tree there taller than about eight or nine feet, and they were all very twisted and gnarled. When we questioned Mike about this, he said that the elephants ate all the new growth, hence the stunted size.

I guess that with only a four-month period in a year when there is any rain, the trees don't get much chance to grow, so it wouldn't take that many elephants to keep the trees well trimmed. The trail we followed wound through these trees. There didn't seem to be more than a few feet of straight trail in any direction making the visibility very limited. Wouldn't you know it, our first rush hour? Traffic jam, and it was wonderful. I never thought that I would be thanking the Lord for something like this, but I did. As we came round another bend, there was a huge herd of elephants crossing the trail one by one or in pairs and small family units, and they were in no hurry. They were not more than twenty feet or so in front of us; it was great, and a fun photo shoot. I have no idea how many there were, but we spent about twenty-five minutes there, watching and photographing these beautiful creatures.

We finally reached the area where the camp was already set up. It wasn't really that far of a drive, but the Lord sure provided for all of us and made for a wonderful day's drive.

09-12-10

Before we came on this blessed trip, I knew that because of the adrenaline rush, I probably would not be able to do much sleeping. Well, in spite of all the excitement, I think I slept for a couple of hours anyway. I'm excited about today's upcoming game drives, but at the same time, I'm kind of sad. Today will already be our last full day in the Moremi.

We had been driving around for about an hour or so with no wildlife sightings other than a couple of stray impala that were not with any herd. Compared to the other game drives, this seemed very strange. In my eyes, the terrain looked perfect for many kinds of game, but there was nothing stirring. Finally as we rounded a sharp bend in the trail, Amy spotted a small bird perched on a shrub branch in a grassy clearing just twenty feet or so away. Mike circled, then stopped so that I could get some shots. It was a little bee-eater, and he was beautiful. It's an overall olive green with yellow throat, black facial markings with a blue tinge in his flight feathers. With the Lord's help, I got some great shots. The bird took off after some insect then returned to the exact spot that he was perched on. As the sun rose a little higher, it warmed up quite a bit. We saw a few more red-billed hornbills, though none were very photogenic, hidden in the brush.

Next we came to another clearing, where there was a fairly large herd of impala grazing on the grasses. A little farther back from the impala, we spotted a pair of warthogs. I was able to get a few photos of the warthogs and impala but nothing to write home about, which is what I'm doing.

We came to a wet marshy area. Mike stopped there for a little break. I didn't see anything moving out here, so while everybody else was out stretching their legs, I kept busy photographing the nearby water lilies in full bloom. I saw a little movement in the reeds. It turned out to be an African jacana; this made for some nice shooting, especially at this close distance. He was beautiful, and with the help of the Lord, I got some nice shots.

The break ended, and Mike said that we were going to go down by the river to scout out that area. The trail is following the river. It's still very bumpy and very twisted. Mike stopped. In the river about forty feet away was a small gaggle, or a flock of geese. These were not our usual Canada geese. These were beautiful Egyptian geese. Medium-sized, tan geese with dark markings and red eyes.

There were five geese here swimming in a tight formation, in good lighting. Thank you, Lord, I got some really good shots. Mike asked me if I had enough shots to satisfy me, and I made the mistake of saying yes before lowering my seat and tightening all the adjustment knobs on my tripod head. He started up so fast that I had to grab the side of the Land Cruiser to balance myself, and the camera flopped over. When I finally got myself and my camera straightened out, we started up again, only to stop again after only a few yards. In front of us about twenty feet away on the trail was a puddle, and on the high ground in the middle was a beautiful malachite kingfisher. He was only about four to five inches tall but a brilliant iridescent blue. There was only one thing wrong with this perfect photo opportunity. I couldn't get my camera to focus or fire. It took me a few minutes to figure out what happened. When the camera flopped over, a little switch on the lens hit the utility frame and switched to the lock position. By the time I found this and flipped the switch, before I could get a shot off, another jeep coming from the other direction scared off the kingfisher. I missed my one chance to photograph this amazing bird that posed so nicely for me.

Missing the chance to get the photographs of the kingfisher and not really seeing any big game made this a very disappointing morning. We were already heading back to camp for brunch and our early afternoon rest period. I prayed for better sightings on this afternoon's game drive.

We arrived back at the camp without seeing any other big game, and I was having very uneasy feelings about this part of the safari. We had our brunch without incident or excitement. After brunch, with Amy's help I scooted out of my chair onto my cot for a very short stretch. I was very anxious because I had noticed that the ground here was not as sandy and was much more solid than at the Xakanaxa camp. Once I was back in my chair, I talked to Mike, and he agreed to allow me the freedom to go wander around a little ways away from the camp in search of photographic subject material. I didn't go very far, probably not more than twenty or thirty yards down toward the river area. The trails out of the camp were still just a little too rough for me to manage in my wheelchair. I was content just to get away from the camp by myself. I was enjoying myself sitting by the water's edge looking around and photographing the scenery and the water lilies. After a while, Mike returned to the camp. He had gotten a radio call from a friend and fellow game driver about a leopard sighting not far from the camp and had gone to check it out. A female leopard had stashed two medium-sized baboon kills in a tree. He found the tree and had been able to see the baboons remains but had not seen the leopard. For our late afternoon/ evening game drive, Mike was taking us to his favorite hippo pool, and the place with the leopard sighting was on the way.

Mike had a special treat for me for that evening. He had brought in another of his small game drive vehicles and Nick, another highly experienced safari driver. Tomorrow Elizabeth and her daughters, Doris and Danielle, would be leaving our group, in this smaller vehicle, to finish their safari in Zambia at Victoria Falls before returning to Switzerland. Mike offered to let me go in this smaller vehicle with Nick and whoever chose to go with me. By going in this smaller jeep, if we found the leopard or anything else and I wanted to stay longer, I could spend more time there and not be subject to pleasing everyone else. Eugenie, the French journalist, chose to go along with me and Nick. Everybody else went with Mike in the larger Land Cruiser. In this jeep, I had room to pull in at an angle behind the driver's seat. At this angle, I could cover two sides instead of the single side that I had been limited to in the larger more crowded Land Cruiser. I was still locked down tight, but by sliding my tripod head along the front bar of my utility frame, I could shoot out the driver's side or the front. It was a quick drive to where the leopard sighting had been. We found the tree where the leopard had stashed her baboon kills, but she was not in the tree.

Mike found the leopard resting on the ground in the light shade near some bushes. Nick pulled in behind and off to the side of Mike so I could get a good angle. I felt blind because I couldn't see the leopard only sixty or seventy feet away. Nick pointed her out, and I couldn't believe that I could have missed her. My God, she was magnificent resting right out in the open. She blended in so well with the grasses as to be almost invisible. Now this was worth the wait and the disappointment of that first two second glimpse of the leopard on the tenth. She was resting on her side and looking around once in a while, unbelievably beautiful. In a short time, Mike left with the group to head to our destination at the hippo pool. I was mesmerized by the beauty of this cat and was having much too much fun photographing this leopard to leave just yet, so Nick pulled up to where Mike had been parked. Now I was only about fifty feet away. I wanted so badly to get out of the jeep and creep closer, just to sit there with her, but Nick wouldn't let me. By now, two other jeeps from another safari concession had pulled up on the opposite side of her about 125 feet behind her. She was getting a little more restless now, head up and looking around more. She had curled her long tail into a perfect single spring-like coil. This was getting more and more perfect. I had my 80–400 mm zoom lens on the camera with a 2x converter, so in essence I had a 160–800 mm zoom lens on.

I had enough shots to allow myself time to experiment by zooming in and out. She was by far the most beautiful creature I had ever seen. She was looking right at me. Great portraits, next she started to yawn, just a little. Still looking straight at me. Another half yawn, just warming up to the real thing. Fantastic, now she had her tail curled up into a single spring-like coil again and has started her real yawn as wide as she can open her mouth, perfect profile. She had raised up the front half of her body into a sphinx-type pose and looked even more beautiful. You could see the power packed into this flawless creature. She was looking around. I was still zoomed in from the yawn shots, and she jumped up into a perfect full profile, and of course, I missed the shot because I couldn't zoom out fast enough. She walked about fifteen feet or so to my right, and then she turned to face me. This was absolutely perfect. She faced me, raised her tail and did her thing, all the while looking straight at me growling with her mouth half open. Then she walked right back, full profile with her tail still coiled up like a spring, to the very spot that she just got up from. Unfortunately, while she was walking back, she had her head turned away, but the photos will speak for themselves. She laid back down and looked like she was out for the count in a deep catnap. This was the highlight of the whole safari. Thank you, Lord. I took 168 photos of the most beautiful creature in the Moremi. After the leopard returned to her catnap, we decided to head out for the hippo pool. My heart was still racing from the adrenaline rush.

To simply see the most elusive cat in all of Africa is a great blessing. To be able to photograph a leopard in the wild, an even greater blessing. To have this magnificent cat virtually perform for me at such a close distance makes me feel so abundantly blessed that I can barely describe it. I only wish that I could say that I did something or acted in such a way that I deserved such a blessing, but I didn't. In fact, I did not deserve any such blessing. I was in a somewhat down mood this morning because I had prayed for, and

I guess, I expected to see and photograph more than just the little bee-eater and the Egyptian geese. I was disappointed because I was thinking about what I didn't get to see and photograph, instead of being thankful for the blessings that the Lord had put right in front of me. I felt like I was ungrateful, so I certainly did not deserve anything else. He blesses us simply because He wants to. Nothing that we can say or do makes us worthy or deserving of any blessings.

We must be ready to receive His blessings, with our hearts and minds on the Lord. It's painfully obvious to me that I was not ready to receive any blessings this morning when He presented me with a perfect malachite kingfisher photo opportunity, and I was unable to get the shot, and I wasted His blessing.

We had only been driving for about fifteen minutes, after leaving the leopard, when we came across a single giraffe among some tall bushes and stunted trees. We stopped for a few minutes, and I took a few photos of the giraffe. While we were stopped I looked around and spotted a shape that I recognized on top of a tree about a hundred or so feet away. Nick identified it as a steppe eagle, and I quickly zoomed in on it and took about a dozen shots. There was no way that we could get any closer because the eagle was across the river. We continued on our way to the hippo pool without any further wildlife sightings.

By the time we arrived at the hippo pool, Mike and the rest of the group were already parked, unloaded, and enjoying the snack treats that Friday, the camp chef, had prepared. Nick parked near the Land Cruiser, and we unloaded and joined the festivities. The area was a gentle clear slope down to the water's edge. The hippo pool was more like a small lake, and there were at least four or five hippos in the nearby water submerging then popping up for air two or three at a time. We all sat around, watching their antics, never knowing where they would pop up next. Unfortunately, the slope was facing north, not an ideal spot for photographing what promised to be a beautiful sunset. I would have much rather have been on the east side of the hippo pool so that we would be facing into the sunset, but the east side was very steep and overgrown and definitely not user friendly. I still took quite a few photos of the beautiful sunset; I just didn't get any hippos in the sunset. I was enjoying photographing the hippos, two or three at a time. As it started to get dark out, the hippos started to spar in the water, mouths wide open, pushing at each other to try to prove their dominance. I was using the flash even though I was really too far away for it to do any good. I just prayed that a few of the shots would come out.

When it was almost too dark to see, Mike said, "Well, the elephants are here." I turned and looked—where did they come from? About 150 feet to our right, a herd of at least twenty-five to thirty elephants had appeared as if by magic. You would think that that many huge elephants would make a lot of noise or that the ground would tremble. But, no, these creatures were absolutely silent in their appearance.

I wanted to get a few photographs, but Mike immediately said, "No flash." I realized why. We were not on the big Land Cruiser but scattered around on the ground with no protection, so it would not be very smart to startle a large group of elephants that were very nearby. We all loaded back up in the dark and headed back to camp.

Thank you, Lord. It had been a fantastic final afternoon/evening of the safari.

09-13-10

I think that I slept better last night than I had the entire safari. After watching and photographing that magnificent leopard, and then watching the hippos antics, I think I was at complete peace. We all loaded up in the Land Cruiser for our final morning game drive and headed out. We did not see much big game that early, but there were plenty of beautiful birds around to keep me busy. Mike headed back toward the area where we had seen the leopard, but she was nowhere to be seen. As we looked around, Mike stopped to point out a greater violet-eared starling. Unlike our starling, which is a European import and, at least in my opinion, not very pretty, this species is quite beautiful with bright iridescent blue patches on the sides of its head. He posed quite nicely for me, and I quickly had my fill of photographs of this bird. We soon came across another lilac-breasted roller poised nicely for me at the very tip of a stunted tree branch not more than ten feet or so of the ground. These turned out to be my best shots of this species from the whole safari. After leaving the roller, we soon came across a lone giraffe grazing among some stunted trees, and even though I had plenty of giraffe photographs, I still took about a dozen more.

Mike headed down toward the river, where we spotted a gray heron in a very shallow muddy area of the river. The gray heron looks very similar to our great blue heron. He was walking around in the shallows looking for food. After I had my fill of photographs, we started up again and only got about fifty yards before Mike stopped again, this time pointing out a small group of about six white-faced ducks. I took a few shots, and then Mike asked me to try to get a shot of them if they took off. As soon as he asked me this the entire flock took off, and I got a couple of poor-quality shots off. We pushed on and came to a large open area with a couple termite mounds.

On the far side of this open area, Mike spotted a couple of ground hornbills and guided the Land Cruiser in for a closer look. These are large turkey-sized birds, rather drab in color with very large bills. The sides of their faces are completely bare of any feathers and bright red in color, and they have a good-sized red bulbous growth on their throat. All in all, it was an interesting but not a very attractive bird. I still took a quite a few shots, and seeing nothing else around, we moved on. Mike headed down to the river where he spotted a couple of hippos in the water, so we stopped to watch for a little while. After I had taken a few hippo shots, I spotted another steppe eagle perched again at the very top of a small tree and took a few shots. We moved on and came across three waterbucks that posed nicely for pictures. After that, there was another small pool in the shallow river where three hippos were very actively playing, and we stopped to watch and photograph. These turned out to be some of my best hippo shots. The water was somewhat shallow, and they were raising their heads and bodies up well out of the water.

It was getting late, so we left the playful hippos and headed back to camp seeing only one lone zebra and a small herd of impala on the way back.

Back at camp, we quickly ate a light lunch that Friday had prepared and then everybody quickly packed up their belongings.

When everything was packed and cleaned up, including the entire camp site, we all gathered in the center area for pictures and to say our good-byes. Elizabeth, Doris, and Danielle were heading north up to Zambia to finish their safari while we headed south to Maun. We gave the crew a good tip and thanked them, knowing that we couldn't have done this safari without their caring help. We then loaded back up into the Land Cruiser and had a long, uneventful drive back to Maun. Since Mike and Sylvia live in Maun most of the year, they both joined us at the Thalamakane Safari lodge for a final dinner at 8:00 p.m. After dinner we all talked for a short time, and then everyone said good-bye and thank you to Mike and Sylvia.

SEPTEMBER 14-17, 2010

On September 14, we packed up, had a quick breakfast, then loaded up into the Mercedes-Benz Sprinter and headed out for the first day journey back to Francistown. Unfortunately, the only wildlife we saw the entire day was a pair of ostriches on the side of the road, and they ran off when we stopped to try to get a few shots. Because of the hotel mess-up in Francistown on the way to Maun, Sylvia changed the reservations, this time to a very nice hotel just across the road from the first disastrous hotel. There were no problems with this hotel, and everybody got a good night sleep without any mishaps.

After breakfast on September 15, we again loaded everything and ourselves back into the Mercedes-Benz Sprinter and started out on the final leg of our journey back to South Africa. Unlike yesterday, today we saw absolutely no wildlife at all the entire way back to Johannesburg. We arrived back at the same beautiful casino hotel near the airport in the early evening, and we all got checked in. At this point, we said good-bye and good luck to Eugenie, the French journalist and her husband Shamus as they headed off on an entirely different journey. They were headed down to Cape Town for a week or so then off to Germany where Shamus was to compose some music for a video of some kind. We were left on our own for the evening. After talking to the hotel manager, they agreed to let us keep the rooms later than the usual check-out times in the morning. Since our flight didn't leave until 5:00 p.m., this allowed me to not be up in my chair for quite as long a stretch because I could get out of my chair and rest until about noon.

September 16, we awoke at the usual time, and I was in my chair by about 6:30 a.m. I cleaned up, brushed my teeth and then just stayed out of the way while Amy and Jackie cleaned up and Amy went through and more or less repacked almost everything before the very long flight back home. We all went down for breakfast at about 8:00 with the luxury of knowing that I could get back out of my chair and stretch until 1:00, when we had to be out of the room. We (Amy, Jackie, myself, Audrey, Cecily, and Charlotte), were all picked up at 3:00 pm for the twenty-minute drive back to the airport.

September 17, the very long flight back to Dulles International in Washington DC was blessedly uneventful. The plane had been full to capacity so when we arrived back at Dulles, it was a while before it was my turn to be taken off the plane. Thank God, this time, my wheelchair was waiting for me right where it should be. Since we had come from Africa, everybody had made a mad dash to customs. In the past, when I have had to go through security or customs, they pulled me off to the side and rushed me through. This time, because we were the last ones off the plane, we were the last in line at the customs, and we were left there unnoticed. There were enough delays that by the time our group got through customs, we had missed our connecting flight to Chicago. The airlines put us on the next available flight, but we had to sit around and wait an extra four hours until that flight. We finally arrived back at O'Hare in Chicago, better late than never. Unfortunately, about half of our group's luggage failed to arrive with us. We spent the next couple of hours with the airport people that handle missing luggage reports.

We finally got home, worried, frustrated, and very tired. Luckily, because I just don't trust the baggage handlers, I always carry my camera gear in my carry-on luggage. Once we arrived back home, in spite of being extremely tired, I started immediately to download my three thousand plus photos from the trip. We received a call later that evening that all our luggage had been found and that they were going to deliver it late that night. Because the delivery needed a signature and they were going to be delivering it at about 1:30 a.m., I arranged with my neighbor to receive the delivery because I had no way to get back out of bed at that hour, and I desperately needed to get out of my chair and stretch out.

All the baggage was there at my neighbor's the next morning to everyone's great relief. This adventure was officially over. Everyone was back home safe and sound with all our luggage and many great memories of a fabulous trip. I immediately started to work on my photos and realized that I already had a desire to go back to Africa again. If it is the Lord's will that I go back someday, I would go in a heartbeat. It's so amazing there.

WHAT AN AWESOME GOD WE HAVE

What an awesome God we have. Only the Creator of the universe could have kept me alive, but not kicking, for this long. Everybody gets older, but not everybody is given less than a 10 percent chance of living one night, just one month after their twenty-eighth birthday. I just celebrated on September 08, 2011, by the grace of God the thirtieth anniversary of my accident. Why did God see fit to give me a second chance? I certainly wasn't worthy of a second chance. Nothing that I ever did in my whole life would make me deserve even the slightest consideration from my Lord and Savior, Jesus Christ. I did everything exactly the opposite of what I should have been doing my whole life. I spent the first fifty years of my life denying that God existed, caught up in a world of science, believing in the theory of evolution with nothing to back it up but what they fed me in school since I was a kid. In spite of the miracle of surviving the accident that by all rights should have killed me, it still took me another twenty-one years before I opened my eyes and saw what a lousy sinner I was and that I needed the forgiveness from the very person that I denied all my life. This world didn't just happen by chance. We didn't just happen by chance. We were created and put here for a reason by somebody far more intelligent and far seeing than us. I am just very thankful that God gave me the time I needed to open my eyes and see the world as it should be seen, knowing where it all came from. I'm glad for the opportunity and grateful for the gifts of the Holy spirit that have allowed me to still get out deep into the wilderness to photograph this magnificent world that He created so that I can share it with others. It's not that my work is that good. It's Look at this magnificent bird, scene, or critter, the Lord created and allowed me to photograph.

Since Christ has been in my life, regardless of the limitations of the wheelchair and the paralysis from my accident, I have seen and done far more with the Lord's guidance than ever before.

Soli Deo gloria. To God alone the glory

EPILOGUE

It's been nearly ten years since that first trip to the Chilkat Valley in Alaska and since I opened my eyes and finally accepted Jesus Christ into my life as my personal Lord and Savior.

There are quite a few places that I would still love to see and photograph in my lifetime. As of now, there are no immediate travel plans for the future. It's been almost three years since the Africa adventure, and I am anxious and willing to go wherever the Lord prompts me to go. If you take that step of faith and decide to follow the Lord with all your heart, you never know where He may send you.

WHEN GOD IS WORKING IN YOUR LIFE

What an amazing feeling it is when God is working in your life. Back in November of 2004, while my photo exhibit was up at the Algonquin Library, Kammren Cusack, an eighteen-year-old Dundee-Crown High School senior was there visiting and talking with me about the photography. Allison Smith had been given the story to write for the *Northwest Herald*. Kammren and I talked about many aspects of photography, and as Allison tells it , "Within minutes, Cusack bent over to hug a smiling, tearful Farber."

This past weekend at the Abilities Expo, while exhibiting my photography, I was visited by a couple from the church I attend, the Calvary Chapel Cardunal. I knew them by face but not their names as they knew me but not my name. After visiting and talking for a while, Karen said that she wanted to show me something. We went behind my screens where she took out a small folded piece of paper and unfolded it. It was the eight-year-old newspaper story that Allison wrote. This couple turned out to be James and Karen Cusack, Kammren's, parents. Kammren is now twenty-six, lives in Florida, and is in the Coast Guard. Karen had found the newspaper story while cleaning out the closet in Kammren's old room. Kammren is coming for a visit this week, and James and Karen are planning on telling him then. It's a very small world. Coincidence? I think not. It's God.

IS IT POSSIBLE?

Is it possible? I'm amazed, and I'm having a hard time believing that in just a few short months, in August, I will be sixty years old. Where did the years go? It still seems like just yesterday that I was twenty-eight, backpacking through the deserts of the southwest and mountain hiking in Glacier National Park in Montana. It also seems like just yesterday, that the doctors gave me less than a 10 percent chance of surviving just one night. Yes, I was in great shape back then, but not good enough to beat those odds. Lucky for me, the Lord had and still has other plans for my life. Most people would think that I would call September 8, 1981, the worse day of my life.

When I think about that day, now almost thirty-two years ago, now that my eyes are open, I believe that it was not the worse day of my life; it probably was the very best thing that could have happened to me at the time. I had been an agnostic from very early in my life, unable to allow myself to believe in anything or anyone other than myself. In my early formative years, I had learned very little of God, and I suppose I had thought of Him in human limitations. How can anybody just create all this beautiful nature. My dad certainly couldn't create anything, I sure couldn't, so how could anybody else? When in school, they presented Darwin's theory of evolution; I grasped that. Here was "proof" of where everything came from. Too bad I didn't know that that "proof" had a fatal flaw, in that it is a false theory. By embracing Darwin's theory plus my own ignorance of God, I was blinded to the real truth.

So for the first fifty years of my life, I walked blindly down that highway of life toward a hellish destination. Only Jesus Christ could have taken what should have been the end of my life and turn it around into a good start of a fruitful life with an eternity in heaven waiting at the end of the road when He decides the time is right to call me home. For somebody in my condition, by following Jesus, I have led a pretty exciting and fulfilling life these past ten years (I was a little slow and reluctant to give up my old way of thinking because it still took me another twenty-two years after my accident to finally open my eyes and accept Jesus Christ into my life and heart as my personal Lord and Savior) because of my love of photographing only His creations. My "walk" with Jesus has taken me to the farthest, most inaccessible reaches of Alaska, to the very edge of the Arctic in Canada, and into the deepest region of Africa's Kalahari Desert. How much more exciting can life on a wheelchair be? All one needs to do is to take that step of faith and be willing to go wherever and whenever you are called to go. I love this life I have been called to lead. I only pray that I can continue to live life to the fullest for His glory.

Soli Deo Gloria.

*Glacier moose This is the photo that I shot 1 year before my accident
in Glacier Nat Park. It's the photo that is hanging on my wall
that helped me get through the bouts of deep depression.*

This steenbok was the first wildlife that we saw crossing the Kalahari in Botswana, Africa.

On Nov 16 2005 in Alaska's Chilkat Valley. A sight I will never forget.

Lilacbreasted roller from Botswana, one of the most colorful birds I have ever seen.

I photographed this male Ruby-throated hummingbird
right outside my bedroom window.

Day 2 in the Wapusk Nat. Park in '07, this polar bear posed by this rock covered with reddish lichens.

This giraffe portrait with two red-billed oxpeckers from Botswana, Africa. I call it "Are you serious".

Eastern bluebird pair photographed at Crabtree Nature
Center in Barrington, IL near my home.

Plains zebras - mare and foal in Botswana Africa.

These three hippos were frolicking in the water in Botswana, Africa.

These three giraffes with necks crossed made it hard for me to see which head went with which body. In Botswana, Africa. I call it who's who.

*This Elephant family unit on my first evening in the
Moremi Game preserve was a real blessing.*

*"Shall we dance" Wapusk Nat. Park these polar bears
decided to put on a wrestling match.*

Dusk on the Wapusk National Park, Canada.

Leopard On my last evening on safari I was blessed to
get within 50 feet of this magnificent leopard.

*The comical look on the eagles face say's to me where do I land
on Nov 16, 2005 in the Chilkat Valley, Alaska.*

This was my favorite Redbilled hornbill shot of this species in Botswana, Africa.

This is the Two bear Katmai sunrise taken on my last morning at the Brooks Camp. The most glorious sunrise I have ever witnessed.

First evening in the Moremi Game Reserve this beautiful sunset behind a herd of Impala.

Day 3 in Botswana from the small boat were in looking up an embankment looking up into the face of an elephant. A wonderful perspective.

On only the sixth and last clear day in all of 2004 Mount McKinley in all her glory.

This Blessed moose was a gift to me from The Lord on our final day in Denali Nat. Park, Alaska.

This eagle posed for photos within minutes of leaving the dock on July 15 2006 in Alaska.

Three tufted puffins on July 15, 2006 in Kenia Fjords Nat. Park.

*Five horned puffins on a rock ledge in the Chiswell Islands
in the Kenia Fjords Nat Park, Alaska.*

Bears fishing the Brooks Falls this one caught a brilliant red Sockeye for her cubs.

This Northern cardinal was resting in my Birch tree after an ice storm.

South Dakota Badlands lightning storm. a single 96 second exposure.

Feb 28, "The Nest" 1997 in Clearwater Florida. I was blessed by seeing this feeding sequence long before I opened my eyes to the truth.

*Lupine Quartet from Brookfield Zoo just after returning
from ther International wolf center in Ely, MN.*

*"Vigilance" My favorite shot from my one trip to the
International wolf Center in Ely, MN.*